This book belongs to

Querida Wally:
Que la lectura de este
librito te acerque a nuestro
Padre Celestial.
Un fuerte abrazo

Olguita
XX

I have been a Christian for most of my life,
but it was only when I started nurturing a little plot of land . . .
that I became acquainted with my Savior.

Through the Seasons with God

A devotional journal for women

OLGA VALDIVIA

Pacific Press®
Publishing Association

Nampa, Idaho | Oshawa, Ontario, Canada
www.pacificpress.com

Designed by Patricia Wegh
Interior illustrations: Gettyimages.com, p. 41 cake by Mary Bausman
Cover design resources from Gettyimages.com

The author assumes full responsibility for the accuracy of all facts and quotations as cited in this book.

You can obtain additional copies of this book by calling toll-free 1-800-765-6955 or by visiting http://www.adventistbookcenter.com.

ISBN: 978-0-8163-6576-0

November 2019

Dedication

To Tessa, Averi, and Elise—
little gleams of sunshine in the garden of my life.

Contents

My Thanks

My infinite thanks to my friend and editor,
Joyce Young,
for her dedication and expertise,
and for challenging and encouraging me
throughout this little journey.
To Patricia Wegh for her dedication
and hours spent in the designing of this project.
To Amanda Withers for her expertise and editing.
And to my heavenly Father,
the Master Gardener,
who ambles through my garden, by my side.
I rest in the mercy of His nearness, and I am free.

Preface

How to Use This Journal

This journal is a devotional about intimacy with God and a keepsake to record your time with your heavenly Father through prayer, praise, and thanks. It is not a daily devotional but a compendium of faith-based messages that cover all four seasons, each with a Scripture verse and many with a sample closing prayer to inspire you.

There are questions with space where you can write what the Holy Spirit stirred in you during your special time with God and what you learned. Having a written record of what God has taught (and is teaching) you becomes a rich source for encouragement during future difficulties. I hope the thoughts in this book and the responses you record provide you with remembrance of how God has worked in your life.

I like to finish each devotional with a prayer and a song of praise to give thanks and honor to the One who is worthy of all praise.

Let's seek the presence of God every day and through each season of our lives.

Give thanks to the LORD, for he is good; his love endures forever.
—Psalm 107:1, NIV

Whenever I run to my favorite place in earnest desire
to have a genuine fellowship with God,
I know I won't be disappointed. I like to think that
my friend Jesus is already there, waiting for me.
—Olga

Introduction

Hello, Friends

I have been a Christian for most of my life, but it was only when I started nurturing a little plot of land that is now a lovely garden that I became acquainted with my Savior, Jesus Christ, and started including Him in my daily life.

Certainly, God shines through nature, and cooperating with it through gardening has given me a completely new perspective on what determines a true relationship with my Savior. You see, it is nearly impossible to open our hearts to the goodness found in nature and remain oblivious to God's love, manifested through His creative power.

> You see, it is nearly impossible to open our hearts to the goodness found in nature and remain oblivious to God's love, manifested through His creative power.

The mockingbirds—those polyglots of the air—voice their songs of many "languages" on flamboyant branches. An Anna's hummingbird, clothed in bright emeralds and blushing jewels, thrills us with fairy-tale dances around the nectar bottles, while over there in the stone fountain, a dozen fat-bellied bluebirds baptize themselves cheerfully.

A swoosh, a swish, a flapping of wings—it is the black-capped chickadee, the yellow western tanager, and the mourning dove, dwellers of the garden. Then, on a wintry morning, out of your peripheral vision comes a flare of wingbeats, and you would know that, again, the red-shafted flicker has found refuge in your garden for another winter.

Soon, breaking the severity of the ice, the early tulips find their way to the surface. Later, the dianthus, the Siberian irises, and waves of daffodils will make their appearances in the garden, summoned by their Creator.

Spring brings the rain. Pure and welcoming rain. We wish for it. We pray for it, and then we hear it, that sudden crack of thunder and the symphony of raindrops, like a glorious song, washing away the pessimism and gloom of the earth, until the sun returns to it again, satisfying it with mirth and goodness.

Summer brings the kiss-me-over-the-garden-gate and Johnny-jump-ups, the lady's-delights, and all the wild pansies. The diminutive sun-faced chamomile flowers shading the feet of the fragrant cloud roses remind us of our Lord's love in diversity. The tall garden phlox, blue larkspurs, and burning nasturtiums, giving way to the canopies of deep-green vines and climbing roses, all speaking of God's amazing creativity and sense of design and attention to detail.

In everything I do in the garden,
everywhere I turn, I find God there.

In everything I do in the garden, everywhere I turn, I find God there. Thus, He has become a dear, close friend with whom I delight in sharing my life. Prayer is a conversation. I talk to my Friend as I work the grounds, as I pull weeds or dig the soil to plant a bulb. He is by my side, watching me, laughing with me, helping me, offering thoughts and advice whenever I am in doubt on what to do about a certain plant or tree.

Whenever I run to my favorite place in earnest desire to have a genuine fellowship with God, I know I won't ever be disappointed. I like to think that my friend Jesus is already there, waiting for me. He rejoices in anticipation of our meeting, and if I ever happen to miss our date, He misses me.

This diary is a humble gathering of thoughts weaved in the midst of a garden I so dearly love. It is not only a tribute to a place, it is also a jamboree of memories and dreams—the whole gifts of my days, perfected in a bouquet of thoughts—my life, exposed for anyone to read.

Olga Valdivia

WELCOME

January

And now we welcome
the new year.
Full of things
that have never been.
—Rainer Maria Rilke

January

A Blank New Page

A new year unfolds upon our lives—a new chapter to be written. A new beginning filled with fragile graces. Optimism rises. Our hopes are renewed. And even when it's not clear, I never doubt that God's promises for our future are unfolding as they should.

Outside my window, the view of the January garden is sweeping and grand. A pure and crystalline newness hangs from trees and bare branches like baubles on a Christmas tree. The atmosphere wears the wings of doves, ashen and soundless. And it seems, too, that the new year moves forward, shrouded in a heavenly cloth decorated in jewels of hope, faith, and sacred gladness.

As the January snows creep in, invited by the slanting winds of winter, the unaccustomed eye may be tempted to see only a garden that has been brutally stripped of its glories. But for the eye that sees far beyond the obvious, there rests genuine loveliness and a chestful of evidences of God's bountiful provisions for humanity at Creation.

The winter garden rejoices in the beauty of frost and the purity of silence. It rests, but it doesn't die. It remains silent, but it still speaks in a thousand voices.

In the bleakness of January, in the barrenness of the land, and in the silence shed by the nude fingers of winter, we can still find joy, beauty, and evidences of God's amazing love toward His children.

Talking to the Father

Father, I am like the winter garden, encrusted in the ice and standoffishness of self-unworthiness and sin. Instead, You saw in me that shining jewel hidden in the ice. You saw value in me. You removed me from the sins that buried me and hindered my light and brought me into life, saved in Your salvation.

Like the new year unfolding before us, so we, Your earthly children, have been given a clean new slate of opportunities. We start anew. May our deeds and lives be witnesses of Your love to those around us from now on.

> Great is his faithfulness; his mercies begin afresh each morning.
> —Lamentations 3:23, NLT

"New Year Resolve"

The time has come
To stop allowing the clutter
To clutter my mind
Like dirty snow,
Shove it off and find
Clear time, clear water.

Time for a change,
Let silence in like a cat
Who has sat at my door
Neither wild nor strange
Hoping for food from my store
And shivering on the mat.

Let silence in.
She will rarely speak or mew,
She will sleep on my bed
And all I have ever been
Either false or true
Will live again in my head.

For it is now or not
As old age silts the stream,
To shove away the clutter,
To untie every knot,
To take the time to dream,
To come back to still water.
—May Sarton

In what ways does the new year renew your hope?

Reflect

∾ As you begin this new year, list some ways you can actively observe God's new mercies each morning.

_____

_____

_____

January

Remember Me

The snow-moistened January garden seems to be whispering, "Remember me?" and, "Who are you?"

Indeed, winter has kept me away from the garden, trapped in its icy grip for far too long. Winter stretches wide and unkind over the land, but the garden is a magnet. I cannot be away from it any longer. It calls me to it; it entices me to render its ground a sacred place of prayer and worship. And as I walk upon its frozen floor this morning, while feeling my head and hands go numb by the tug of icy winds, I am nevertheless pulled to it with renewed enthusiasm.

I want to obey these feelings in my heart and begin working the soil. I want to sow a thousand seeds and start dividing the hostas, but the gusts of icy wind that scatter restless leaves around my feet reaffirm in me the notion that this is only January. I must wait.

My eyes study the silent garden: its rugged nakedness, the ashen shades of January painting its quiet anatomy with the sorrows of the graveyard, and I am inexorably reminded of my own fate.

Each fallen leaf and bare tree limb, the vanished perennials of yesterdays, and every needle, snag, and organic debris accumulating on the garden's floor are all brutal tokens of finitude and hopelessness. They shout,

> "You [shall] return to the ground,
> for out of it you were taken;
> for you are dust,
> and to dust you shall return" (Genesis 3:19, ESV).

God is our secure place of refuge.

The sense of impermanence is overwhelming. But then, as if a reminder that our home and ultimate destination is heaven, from my peripheral vision suddenly erupts the sight of gentle, velvety light, emanating from the hurri-

> You are my refuge
> and my shield;
> I have put my hope
> in your word.
> —Psalm 119:114, NIV

cane lamp sitting by my kitchen window.

Light coming in threads of unpretentious coppery gold. Light melting the gloominess of my thoughts and reminding me that home is where my refuge and comfort reside. A burnished glow flowing like honey all over my soul, and my spirit is quickly revived with optimism and renewed faith.

My warm, illuminated home is a reminder of God's promises. He is home. He is home to the weary of this world. He is the Light from which humanity derives life. He is our secure place of refuge from the inclemency of our human existence. Our fortress in time of trouble and the Master of our fate.

My mind has been quieted; my heart assured.

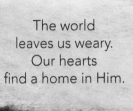

The world leaves us weary. Our hearts find a home in Him.

Talking to the Father

Father, how very precious and life-giving Your promises are. I have grown weary with years and fearful by what lies before me, but I will not be guided by feelings but by Your constant love and unwavering promises of hope and eternal life.

God's Words

"For as in Adam all die, even so in Christ shall all be made alive" (1 Corinthians 15:22, KJV).

Reflect

∾ Spend some time reflecting on how God as led you in the past. How does this change the way you see today and the future?

_____

_____

_____

_____

_____

January

The Winter Garden

We woke up this morning to an amalgamation of fog and solid frost. Frost on rooftops and street lights. Frost on dried leaves scattered on solidified grass and on roses crystallized like candies.

I can hardly see the junipers just down the garden past the fence, muffled as they are under this silent cloud of muted whites and grays. There are no caroling birds to serenade the morning. No petals embellishing the pea-gravel paths. Yet the garden is overflowing with countless quiet blessings:

- The purity of ice-covered mornings and crispness on frozen wings of the atmosphere.
- The holy silence born only in the depths of winter.
- The gentleness in which nature repairs the landscape and all its surfaces.
- The times winter breezes carry nature's jewels from the frozen land into the house—a dried leaf, like little waves of incense satisfying my soul with assurance, love, and peace—all gifts from God.

The austerities of the winter garden remind me that adversity and trials, when left under the divine care of God, become blessings in disguise. "Not only that, but we rejoice in our sufferings, knowing that suffering produces endurance, and endurance produces character, and character produces hope, and hope does not put us to shame, because God's love has been poured into our hearts through the Holy Spirit who has been given to us" (Romans 5:3–5, ESV).

Spring follows the darkest days of winter.

It is easy to lose hope in the wintry garden. It is easy to forget that spring follows the darkest days of winter. Uncertainty and doubt can fill our hearts with fear when there seems to be no way out. But for the true Christian, that's usually when God's presence shines the brightest.

Talking to the Father

Father, "make me an instrument of Thy peace; where there is hatred, let me sow love; where there is injury, pardon; where there is doubt, faith; where there is despair, hope; where there is darkness, light; and where there is sadness, joy.

"O, Divine Master, grant that I may not so much seek to be consoled, as to console; to be understood, as to understand; to be loved, as to love; for it is in giving that we receive, it is in pardoning that we are pardoned, and it is in dying that we are born again to eternal life."*

Reflect

ᕚ List some of your favorite winter blessings that remind you of God's presence.

_____

_____

ᕚ Recall a time when God used winter to restore your hope.

_____

_____

> God's presence shines brightest in the darkness.

God's Words

"And the peace of God, which surpasses all understanding, will guard your hearts and your minds in Christ Jesus" (Philippians 4:7, ESV).

_____

* This anonymous text is usually called the "Prayer of Saint Francis" or "Peace Prayer."

January

Time Has Wings

> He will cover you with
> his feathers.
> He will shelter you with
> his wings.
> His faithful promises
> are your armor
> and protection.
> —Psalm 91:4, NLT

Time has wings. Time is a bird, and we are the small riders on its back, holding on to it with fists full of feathers that are our days and years.

Our eyes are teary with the winds of our burdens. Our days are measured in wingbeats that bring us trials and despair as well as growth and opportunities.

If time possesses wings, then our spirit must soar in God's perspective of time. For we are dust, but God is timeless. Our lives are short and frail; however, God does not weaken or fail with the passage of time. There is no before and after in Him. There is no time at which He is not.

I like how the psalmist reveals the protective aspect of God's character with the idea of God wanting to gather us under His wings. If time is a bird, then I want to ride under the wings of the Almighty.

Lord, my days are all in the hollow of Your hands.

Talking to the Father

O God, we are swept away by our years as with a flood. We are like a dream, like grass that flourishes in the morning and in the evening fades and withers. But You, O God, transcend time. You are above and outside the sphere of our time. You are the light that guides our trembling steps and infuses us with inner peace and harmony that can follow us throughout our limited life.

Lord, my days are all in the hollow of Your hands.

"Under His Wings"

Under His wings I am safely abiding;
Though the night deepens and tempests are wild,
Still I can trust Him; I know He will keep me;
He has redeemed me, and I am His child.
Under His wings, under His wings.
—W. O. Cushing

God's Words

"Like an eagle that stirs up its nest,
   that flutters over its young,
spreading out its wings, catching them,
   bearing them on its pinions"
(Deuteronomy 32:11, ESV).

Reflect

ა What is God asking you to do
with the time He gives you
today?

_____

_____

_____

_____

_____

January

Wings in the Wind

For many, the first sight of an American robin foraging for food among the ashen grass of late winter is a sign that spring is close by. But is winter really gone? And are those orange-breasted feathered friends of the garden genuine harbingers of spring, or are they not? One must wonder.

Winter has kept us firm in its grip with temperatures well below freezing, and the weak sun of January has no power to purge the land of old snows. Even as I write, a powdery whisper of winter dust is gently sprinkling us in a faint, damped murmur. We walk into the deepest dwellings of winter, and yet nature insists in finding ways to amaze us with wonder beyond reasoning.

Early this morning, the sky was overshadowed by a large flock of robins that soon took possession of our neighborhood. They found the garden, and they at once engaged in a ruckus wintertime festivity that had kept my thoughts alive with wonderment and excitement since then.

> We walk into the deepest dwellings of winter,
> and yet nature insists in finding ways to amaze us
> with wonder beyond reasoning.

As this social gathering got louder and louder, I watched in astonishment at how those birds jockeyed for position on tree branches, devouring the fruit of the crab apple trees and the hackberries, then dashed down to the snow-covered ground for an additional meal of earthworms, and back again to the trees.

Perhaps arriving too early in the season to have returned to our northern regions, they looked to me more like some lost wanderers of the earth than the true migrants they are. Acrobats and performers of some great traveling circus, they were clad in their vibrant orange flocks and suits in gradients of midnight black.

I marveled as I observed these little creatures of the air, and I thanked our Creator for their fancy appearance and graces so intricate and skillful.

My reverie lasted until, finally, the afternoon lights became dim, and the little trapeze artists and flamenco dancers were gone, leaving the garden once again as empty and quiet as before the soiree began. And I was left alone to ponder and meditate on God's inscrutable ways.

Talking to the Father
Father, Your inventiveness and inspiration at Creation never cease to amaze me. Your resourcefulness and vision are yet another confirmation that You, and only You, are Lord.

God's Words
"But ask now the beasts, and they shall teach thee; and the fowls of the air, and they shall tell thee" (Job 12:7, KJV).

Reflect
∾ In what ways is God revealing His character to you?

January

When Faith Weakens

Days are lengthening. Shadows diminishing. The changes taking place in nature are almost imperceptible. While the sun's orbit has been slowly climbing as the length of daylight increases, changes up to this point have been relatively subtle. Nonetheless, the nature lover knows better; the eye sees, the heart knows, and already my wings are fluttering with spring songs. I'm the little bird dreaming of waves of golden daffodils and clusters of flame-red tulips.

My heart is eager for long walks and dappled sunlight scattered among tall grasses. And whose would not be!

I am ready for days of diamond-like light shining atop tepid waters, ready for birds singing on flowering branches, and mourning doves building flimsy platforms made of twigs and pine needles in the prickly branches of the Sally Holmes roses. And as I drink in my mind pictures of spring, I'm imbued with a surge of anticipation and excitement. My energies are revived as if warm, sunny breezes were already blowing on my face.

While the bitterness of winter, with its assistants, ice and snow, is still the same, I know there will always be spring. This is no figment of my imagination, no fantasy. Rivers will flow again after being frozen for long months, and roses will grow again on frostbitten branches.

> The process and continuity of the seasons
> help us remember that God is there.

On those days when faith weakens and we cannot see God, the process and continuity of the seasons help us remember that God is there; He is the same yesterday and today and forever. He is not an idea made up by the simpleminded. He is not a reflection of our desire to believe the impossible. He is the God of all possibilities.

> For the invisible things of him from the creation of the world are clearly seen, being understood by the things that are made, even his eternal power and Godhead; so that they are without excuse.
> —Romans 1:20, KJV

The apostle Peter knew in his heart what it is to be imbued with the anticipation and excitement of seeing God: "Though you have not seen him, you love him; and even though you do not see him now, you believe in him and are filled with an inexpressible and glorious joy" (1 Peter 1:8, NIV).

Hidden right in the middle of my winter's tale is a gift that I should receive in total sincerity and humility and full awareness of its value. We may not perceive God's presence in the midst of today's challenge, but He is as real as spring and as true as all seasons.

Be of good cheer. After the frost of trials and sufferings, there comes a spring of eternal joy.

"Unchangeable, All-Perfect Lord"

Unchangeable, all-perfect Lord!
Essential life's unbounded sea!
What lives and moves, lives by Thy word;
It lives, and moves, and is, from Thee!
Whate'er in earth, or sea, or sky,
Or shuns, or meets, the wandering thought,
Escapes, or strikes, the searching eye,
By Thee was to existence brought.
—Ernst Lange; translated by John Wesley

> His promises are unchanging and trustworthy.

God's Words
"For now we see only a reflection as in a mirror; then we shall see face to face. Now I know in part; then I shall know fully, even as I am fully known" (1 Corinthians 13:12, NIV).

Reflect
ꙮ What is God using to renew your faith?

_____

_____

_____

_____

_____

January

Winter Blues

White is the color of the land. White drapes itself onto the bleakness beyond my window, mingling into one with the wide, lazily looping snow-flakes drifting down in unpredictable directions on the whims of the winds. White covers roofs and naked branches, and it is also the lackluster land-scape of my spring-colored soul.

By this time of the year, winter blues have set in deep. I find it hard to acclimatize to my surroundings, and I am feeling the nicks and marks of the season's frozen fingers over my days with a bitter heart.

A cold wind blows from somewhere all over the garden, and I think I see the trees shivering under their white quilt. I had to wonder what gives trees the strength to endure ruthless winter conditions, which bend and distort their beautiful forms. And then, I see it: a wonderful future beckons and winks at me.

"For the Lord God will give them light."

Just like the trees, we have a future. And yes, there is a glorious tree in our ultimate future, a tree like no other:

On each side of the river stood the tree of life, bearing twelve crops of fruit, yielding its fruit every month. And the leaves of the tree are for the healing of the nations. No longer will there be any curse. The throne of God and of the Lamb will be in the city, and his servants will serve him. They will see his face, and his name will be on their foreheads. There will be no more night. They will not need the light of a lamp or the light of the sun, for the Lord God will give them light. And they will reign for ever and ever (Revelation 22:2–5, NIV).

> May the God of hope fill you with all joy and peace in believing, so that by the power of the Holy Spirit you may abound in hope.
> —Romans 15:13, ESV

God's Silence

There are no birds to be seen. No fluttering of wings or cooing of doves to be heard. No sounds of little creatures scurrying among dried grass and pea-gravel paths. Nothing breathes. Steady silence settles and hovers over the winter-dampened garden.

The emptied silence that broods over the land at the heart of winter frightens me at times. It reminds me of God's dreadful silence when our hearts are desperate for words.

What do we make of God's silence? And why does our heart seek to hear Him speak? We were born to communicate. Language is an essential part of our human existence.

David knew firsthand what it is to hunger for a word from God:

> As the deer pants for streams of water,
>   so my soul pants for you, my God.
> My soul thirsts for God, for the living God. . . .
> My tears have been my food
>   day and night,
> while people say to me all day long,
>   "Where is your God?" (Psalm 42:1–3, NIV).

I can only imagine the depths of David's frustrations that pushed him to tears. So much so that those around him say, "Where is this God of yours that you pray to?"

But as we read further in the psalm, we realize that David will not remain in despair. He speaks to himself out of his deep relationship with God:

> As the deer pants
> for streams of water,
> so my soul pants
> for you, my God.
> —Psalm 42:1, NIV

29

Why, my soul, are you downcast?
    Why so disturbed within me?
Put your hope in God,
    for I will yet praise him,
        my Savior and my God (verse 5, NIV).

Is God truly silent? Satan appeals to human logic by trying to get us to project our human perceptions onto God; he pushes us to believe that God's silence means He doesn't care or doesn't loves us.

> "Perhaps it's not silence we're encountering
> while we seek God, but rather a pregnant pause."

I like how James Emery White, PhD, in his book *Wrestling With God* puts it, "Perhaps it's not silence we're encountering while we seek God, but rather a pregnant pause—a prompting to engage in personal reflection so that the deepest of answers, the most profound of responses, can be given and received."

Winter provides the silence I need in order to listen. And so does God.

Talking to the Father

Dear heavenly Father, I am feeling weighed down by the plethora of silent waters of life. Teach me, O Lord, to behold Your face in Your apparent silence, that I may rise above my incredulities and rest assured in Thy faithfulness. For my heart is deaf to Your voice and blind to Your nearness.

Reflect

ᐁ How will I respond when God seems silent?

_____

_____

_____

_____

_____

God
is there
even in the silence.

The Pure Light of His Love

An unusual brightness woke me up from deep sleep rather early this morning. The sun hadn't come up yet, but already the room was aglow with a buoyant luster that could only mean one thing: snow!

I ran to look outside, not wanting to miss a moment. Excitement ran through my veins. From the window of our second-floor room, the world below was pale and bright, covered under thick cottony blankets.

Ice infiltrated the edges of the window as snow blew in the wind. Big, fluffy flakes swirled and soared like miniature birds, each competing against another as if in the quest to set a record. I had the sensation of looking through a snow globe.

As predawn light emerged, casting a gloomy bluish hue over the wintry landscape, the white expanse outside my "snow-covered globe" seemed to have grown larger and lonelier. An overwhelming feeling of joy came over me and filled my heart with contentment. Today, God was looking into the snow globe of our planet and smiling. The pure light of His love was again finding its way into my world. I was not alone in my winter garden. I found myself praising His name for the brief beauty of snowflakes playing outside my window and the warmth of His presence in my heart.

He says to the snow,
"Fall on the earth,"
and to the rain shower,
"Be a mighty downpour."
—Job 37:6, NIV

Talking to the Father
Father, thanks for the white, bright mornings of our soul, when Your Spirit blinds us with Your beauty and our heart overflows with Your presence.

Reflect
ᴥ How do you maintain your focus on God in times of discouragement?

_____

_____

God's Words
"So do not fear, for I am with you" (Isaiah 41:10, NIV).

January

The Miracle of Light

We have been gifted by the snow of yesterday with a gentle, fair-haired maiden of a landscape this morning. A strong sun reposes over the snow-covered garden, where every tree and every tree branch wears new frocks of twinkling stars.

Bushes and old roses are clothed in gems of the purest of bright whites, and birds have invited themselves over to the soiree under sunny blue skies. They are everywhere, twirling and whirling with a renewed happiness that's almost tangible. They remind me of children playing outside on a snowy day.

Do birds get to make their own snow birds? Do they shape little white robins and chickadees with fluffy snow and small twigs? I've never seen one, but I wouldn't be surprised if they did.

Sunshine, indeed, is a welcome thing. I am in awe at the miracle of light and at how my spirit is lifted, like with the birds in the garden, when touched by the sun.

Father, You are the keeper of all creation.

I stand in awe before God's gift of brightness and energy. I marvel at the power that moved above the waters and filled the earth with warmth, hope, and happiness at Creation and repeats the miracle every day, everywhere on our planet.

Talking to the Father

Father, only You can create true energy and light and life. Your treasures are all around us, in plain view. You are the Keeper of all creation, and the Proprietor of my heart.

WELCOME

February

Winter is the time for comfort,
for good food and warmth,
for the touch of a friendly hand
and for a talk beside the fire:
it is the time for home.
—Edith Sitwell

Whatever Is Lovely

Few things are more exciting to me than sleeping in the garden on a summer's day. The feelings are those similar to walking in a meadow of tiny flowers sprinkled with stardust, or strolling through fields of dazzling Queen Anne's lace, and going back in time to find the little puffball-pink clover flowers that glittered above the pasture where I grew up.

Waking up under the canopy of trees that shrouds my little sanctuary is like being part of a fairy tale written by God. But this is only February, and the garden has time yet to cuddle down deeper into winter's icy covers. I'll have to wait for those pleasures during the summer.

The Lord is not slow in keeping his promise, as some understand slowness. Instead he is patient with you, not wanting anyone to perish, but everyone to come to repentance. .
—2 Peter 3:9, NIV

His promises are unchanging and trustworthy.

As wonderful as February is, it is an "in-between" month, still filled with winter's cold wonder, and already teasing us with slightly warmer days. We decide how we will feel about February. We can embrace the opportunity it gives, as Edith Sitwell wrote, for "good food and warmth, for the touch of a friendly hand and for a talk beside the fire."

Faith in God's promises gives us a better outlook for the future and a more positive concept of the present. Happiness is indeed a state of mind bolstered in the Christian by the peace instilled in our hearts by God's promises.

Talking to the Father
Lord, please help me give You any gloomy thoughts and situations that are out of my control, and help me remember Your promises, so I won't be pushed around by the fears in my mind.

God's Words
"Finally, brothers, whatever is true, whatever is honorable, whatever is just, whatever is pure, whatever is lovely, whatever is commendable, if there is any excellence, if there is anything worthy of praise, think about these things" (Philippians 4:8, ESV).

February

Beauty Is a Light in the Heart

I love it when, all of a sudden, one day in the heart of winter, birds invade your garden and you have to stop whatever it is you're doing and simply watch and stand amazed.

Of course, it just wasn't any kind of bird. It was the red-winged blackbird—a whole flock of them. That Sabbath they stayed all day long. And such a scene they made in the garden, feeding on frost-ripened fruits, hastening from the crab apple trees to the American holly to the dogwood berries and back again to the crab apples; beautifully assenting our Creator's legacy of beauty and love toward our small world.

I like to think that as these birds were heading to a more placid, warmer place, they looked down, and on discovering our little garden decided to make a short stop before continuing on their long journey. What a happy thought that was!

The red-winged blackbird is one of my favorite birds. But not exactly for qualities of extraordinary beauty. Black adult males' red shoulder patches are the only indication of color on these birds, mainly visible only when the bird is flying or displaying. Females and young ones are even less interesting in their appearance—a streaky brown, mostly resembling a large, dark sparrow.

There is nothing interesting about the appearance of the red-winged blackbird. But I find these birds were gifted with a uniquely lovely song, like no other bird. The soothing song these birds emit—the *conk-la-ree* that starts with an abrupt note that turns into a musical trill—truly captivates the spirit.

Do these birds remind you of someone you know?

I like how Lebanese American poet and writer Kahlil Gibran puts it: "Beauty is not in the face; beauty is a light in the heart."

Talking to the Father

Father, remind me that "charm is deceptive, and beauty is fleeting; but a woman who fears the Lord is to be praised" (Proverbs 31:30, NIV).

The Touch-Me-Nots

My heart yearns for the seclusion of the Christian hermit and the interior detachment and solitude that brings spiritual growth and prayer.

If I could choose the perfect dwelling place of my heart, no doubt I would choose the shelter of the garden, with only the black-winged tanager for a friend and the wail of the mourning dove for company.

Going through the pages of some of my old journals this morning, I realized, with certain sadness, how often I have tried to express the flow of my feelings through my writings. Sentiments expressed on different days of different years, written with different words, but still the core of emotions remains the same.

Am I, in my quest for solitude and a deeper relationship with God, perhaps imitating those Christians who misinterpret what Jesus was trying to convey when He said that we are to be in the world but not of the world?

It's relatively easy to find Christians who separate themselves from the rest of the world under the pretense of zeal for God. These Christians remind me of the spotted touch-me-nots, wildflowers that sometimes grow rampant among the weeds. These interesting little flowers get their names from their explosive characteristic. At the slightest pressure, the ready seedpods explode, shooting seeds in all directions.

The human heart is the most deceitful of all things, and desperately wicked. Who really knows how bad it is?
—Jeremiah 17:9, NLT

Without love, we are nothing.

These are the "touch-me-not" Christians of today. "Touch me not, people! I don't desire your company or your friendship. I don't desire having to deal with you or care to hear about you. Touch me not, God! Do not ask me to reach out to those who do not deserve goodness and kindness. I'm satisfied where I am planted. Happy in my own protected little world, trying to become the Christian You want me to be. Don't bother to call me to the sacrificial life, Lord. Touch me not."

The fact is, God does wants us to be very much involved in the lives of those around us. He asks us to be actively and properly involved *in* the world so we can reach and help others, while at the same time making sure we do not participate in the evil, depravity, and corruptness *of* this world.

It is good to desire a deeper relationship with God through solitude and prayer. But it is not OK to forget that, without love, we are nothing (1 Corinthians 13:2).

Ellen White wrote in *Steps to Christ*:

"God is love" is written upon every opening bud, upon every spire of springing grass. The lovely birds making the air vocal with their happy songs, the delicately tinted flowers in their perfection perfuming the air, the lofty trees of the forest with their rich foliage of living green—all testify to the tender, fatherly care of our God and to His desire to make His children happy. . . .

God has bound our hearts to Him by unnumbered tokens in heaven and in earth. Through the things of nature, and the deepest and tenderest earthly ties that human hearts can know, He has sought to reveal Himself to us (page 10).

Talking to the Father
Dear Lord, abide in me that I may be filled with Your perfect love.

Reflect
ꙮ How do I balance living *in* the world, without becoming *of* the world?

_____

_____

ꙮ What steps do (or can) I take to daily abide in Christ?

_____

_____

God's Words
"If I have the gift of prophecy and can fathom all mysteries and all knowledge, and if I have a faith that can move mountains, but do not have love, I am nothing" (1 Corinthians 13:2, NIV).

God shares His love with us through nature's beauty.

February

Spiritual Warfare

Yesterday, late afternoon, a most unequal battle took place in the garden between a large Cooper's hawk and a small junco. It was a poignant incident that kept me thinking about it for days.

I heard the eerie call piercing the crisp February air and immediately knew what it was. The hawk flew high above the garden in a serene flap-flap-glide pattern for a while, waiting, practicing patience and persistence. Then, the large bird's flying pattern changed abruptly. It circled the air in a faster, lower pattern, and it zoomed to the ground almost in a frenzy.

A whirlwind of feathers in streaks of brown and white shadowed the garden's floor for a split second. It was hard to tell what was going on, until I saw the hawk take perch atop a large tree stump and begin its meal.

Before I realized what had happened, the hawk had seized up the junco and made a clean kill. The small creature did not have a chance.

I couldn't help seeing what had just transpired as a reflection of our own humanity and our struggle with the enemy of our soul. The Bible tells us that Satan has had a strategic plan from the beginning of time to deceive and destroy humankind. We are engaged in spiritual warfare. If we fix our attention on our inadequacies and faults, we are but a trembling junco under Satan's attacks. Thankfully, we serve a God who is far stronger than Satan. Satan's power is limited; God's power is limitless. Satan's power is temporary; God's power is eternal.

> And surely I am with you always, to the very end of the age.
> —Matthew 28:20, NIV

Talking to the Father

Lord, I am a weak junco struggling for survival. I am soon to succumb if not for Your help. I need the spiritual armor that comes from an unbroken companionship with You.

God's Words

"Dear friends, now we are children of God, and what we will be has not yet been made known. But we know that when Christ appears, we shall be like him, for we shall see him as he is" (1 John 3:2, NIV).

February

My Strength Is Trust

I look out the window and see it every day—our stout ponderosa pine tree—enduring the tantrums of the seasons and threatening to overpower our suburban yard. It is a master of strong winds, rain, and blazing heat.

Trees amaze me. Their stout strength and perseverance speak to my heart in special ways. Winds can steal their leaves, snap their boughs, and peel off their bark. Snows can bend their shape, and heat scorches their branches, but trees still hold their ground.

The secret of their strength resides in the roots. Roots, stretched in the womb of the earth, are safe. They cannot be touched. They silently, invisibly, determine the tree's future.

Talking to the Father

Father, You have given us the strength of trees. Beneath the brittle, frayed edges of our bark, Your hand sustains us. The winds of trials can bend us, but we will not break if You are by our side. We are only able to stand up to the winds that whip us if You hold us fast under the shadow of Your wings. You have comforted us, shaded us with Your peace. We are throwing our dreams into space like a kite, Lord. We don't know exactly what the breezes of life will bring back, but if You continue to guide us as You have always done, we know with certainty we're heading toward the growing light of the day.

Author Hermann Hesse wrote, "When we are stricken and cannot bear our lives any longer, then a tree has something to say to us: Be still! Be still! Look at me! Life is not easy, life is not difficult. Those are childish thoughts. Let God speak within you, and your thoughts will grow silent. You are anxious because your path leads away from mother and home. But every step and every day lead you back again to the mother. Home is neither here nor there. Home is within you, or home is nowhere at all."

A Coconut-Glazed Cake

We woke up this morning to a powdered-sugar sprinkle of light snow. The garden looks like a coconut-glazed cake. I suspect this may be the work of angels. Perhaps some mischievous angels passing by during the early hours of morning looked down and, upon discovering our bare winter garden, decided it was a Bundt cake ready to be glazed? And the garden looks glorious this morning under its snow-drizzled glaze, which is dripping down the sides.

Does God intend to provide these wonderful extras? I know He does. God loves to amaze us with His sense of humor and wonder. We only have to look at some of God's creations to know He does.

Check out the gerenuk of eastern Africa, with its giraffe-like neck on a body of a gazelle, for example. Or take a long look at the rectangular pupils of goats or the toothless mouths of turtles. Closer to home, we are delighted by the clumsiness of puppies, the hugeness of sunflowers, and beards on cornstalks. This diversity, such richness of detail, comes from an amazingly capable and creative God.

I see God's sense of humor throughout the Bible. A donkey who spoke with the voice of the living God overmatches Balaam, who claimed to have prophetic speech. What a terrific way God chose to teach Balaam a lesson in humility. And how funny!

Whether we are seeing snow that looks like coconut glaze, bathing chickadees, or gravity-defying hummingbirds, God is everywhere, delighting us with the wonders of His creation.

> Then our mouth was filled with laughter, and our tongue with shouts of joy; then they said among the nations, "The LORD has done great things for them."
> —Psalm 126:2, ESV

God's Words
"Be glad in the LORD, and rejoice, O righteous, and shout for joy, all you upright in heart!" (Psalm 32:11, ESV).

February

The Silvery Light of the Moon

My shadow follows the silvery light of the moon as I fumble my way around in the gloominess of the sleepy house. From my kitchen window I follow the round silhouette gliding the early sky, guessing where her hiding place may be.

> The heavens declare the glory of God; the skies proclaim the work of his hands.
> —Psalm 19:1, NIV

As I sit by the table with my Bible and books minutes later, she's still out there, illuminating the gloominess outside. A few more minutes, however, and the anatomy of the sky has already shifted. The moon seems less bright now, perhaps less pompous in her beauty, resembling the old danseuse who, knowing her time is past, surrenders her life's dreams to the inexorable wheels of time. The firmament is the dancing floor where, clad in her mortuary regalia, the moon performs her last dance to the tune of the early dawn.

This miracle—this intertwining of night and day, of moon and sun, silvery light softly fading into bright globules of light—takes place so quickly that if you are not paying close attention, you'll miss it. The entire swift, miraculous moment of transition between night and day will dissolve into nothingness, leaving us hungering for a recurrence for far too long.

I always think of this moment of transition as a calling song from God. He moves from lyric to lyric, from chord to chord, until His song is either heard or ignored. Our heavenly Father delights in a relationship with His children. He is constantly offering His direction. His voice is louder than our fears and vulnerabilities, but we've been given options. His song for intimacy, if accepted, will become our hymn of victory. But if we continually ignore it, the notes will become quieter and quieter and quieter . . .

God's Words

"The gatekeeper opens the gate for him, and the sheep listen to his voice. He calls his own sheep by name and leads them out. When he has brought out all his own, he goes on ahead of them, and his sheep follow him because they know his voice. But they will never follow a stranger; in fact, they will run away from him because they do not recognize a stranger's voice" (John 10:3–5, NIV).

I Am With You Always

To walk through the solitary winter garden brings to the imagination a walk through the mystical landscape of poetry. I will reach a certain shady corner that mimics the pages of some mystery book, where dark, damp winds drag stories around and frail naked branches snap under bitter wintry winds, as trees sway back and forth, moved by silent natural forces, and deadwood creaks, sending off false sounds of doors opening and closing.

And surely
I am with you always,
to the very end
of the age.
—Matthew 28:20, NIV

Sometimes my garden takes me into the fantastic world of ancient journeys as I walk on a carpet of dead leaves and look to remaining tangles of grapevines and cold brown branches. There are the burning bushes and barberries reaching out to scratch me, telling me to stay out of their space.

I love every segment of my garden in every season, but there is something far more beautiful and powerful than the inspiration a garden has to offer, and that's what brings me here, even on the harshest day of winter.

> Beyond the poetic beauty of a living garden,
> there resides the imperceptible
> yet sometimes overpowering presence of God

You see, beyond the poetic beauty of a living garden, there resides the imperceptible yet sometimes overpowering presence of God. The Holy Spirit reaffirms this notion: "The LORD your God will be with you wherever you go" (Joshua 1:9, NIV).

It is true that God is to be found anywhere and everywhere, but there is something about a garden that speaks to my soul like no other place. English poet and hymnist Dorothy Frances Gurney shared my sentiments when she wrote:

The kiss of the sun for pardon,
The song of the birds for mirth,
One is nearer God's Heart in a garden
Than anywhere else on earth.

In harmony and peacefulness, in goodness and assurance, God's presence is always comforting us, moving us to desire a closer relationship with Him. God's walk with His earthly children is not a short-term compromise. It is an all-year walk. He is with us in the winter garden of our lives just as He positively walks by our sides during delicious spring days, balmy summer evenings, and glorious autumn days. He is with us through the good times and the bad. He is a never-changing God. Circumstances or influences that cause change in our lives have no effect on Him.

Talking to the Father
My soul clings to You, O Lord, for in You I trust.

Reflect
❧ In what ways is God comforting me today?

_____

_____

_____

❧ Make a list of ways God has demonstrated His presence in your past experiences.

_____

_____

_____

God walks
with me
and talks with me.

The kiss of sun for pardon,
the song of the birds for mirth,
one is nearer God's heart in a garden
than anywhere else on earth.
—Dorothy Frances Gurney

WELCOME

March

*How many lessons of faith and beauty
we should lose, if there were no winter in our year!*
—Thomas Wentworth Higginson

March

Trials Are Just Like Fog

For our light
and momentary troubles
are achieving for us
an eternal glory that far
outweighs them all.
—2 Corinthians 4:17, NIV

The fine but relentless drift of a rain that took place late yesterday evening gave way to the damp sheets of fog that have transformed the scope of my little world outside the window this morning. But the new day still has some promises to reveal.

Fog assures me of a gentle sun, and the eventual lifting of shadows, the vanishing of this colorless miasma where sky, land, and garden are one and the same under the unyielding whims of early March. Fog is always temporary; that's why it reminds me of my trials and tribulations. It calls me to expect something better, sooner or later.

"In all this you greatly rejoice, though now for a little while you may have had to suffer grief in all kinds of trials" (1 Peter 1:6, NIV). The fisherman from Galilee, Peter, reminds us that our trials, just like fog, are temporary. God permits our trials for a purpose. They prove the genuineness of our faith and dependence on God. Soon the Light of the world, our Savior, Jesus Christ, will appear through the darkest clouds of our existence, piercing them with His presence, decadence, and death. Like the sun dissipates fog, Christ will erase our trials from our memory forevermore.

It is encouraging to discover that some of the most beautiful hymns in the history of Christianity were composed through pain and difficult experiences. Horatio Spafford wrote the unforgettable hymn "It Is Well With My Soul" after his three daughters drowned in a shipwreck:

> When peace, like a river, attendeth my way,
> When sorrows like sea billows roll—
> Whatever my lot, Thou hast taught me to say,
> It is well, it is well with my soul.
> It is well with my soul,
> It is well, it is well with my soul.

Perhaps we fail to realize that with the trials and tribulations there comes a new understanding of the grace of God.

Horatio Spafford wrote, "For me, be it Christ, be it Christ hence to live: If Jordan above me shall roll, no pang shall be mine, for in death as in life Thou wilt whisper Thy peace to my soul."

Reflect

ᴥ What lessons am I learning about God through my trials?

_____

_____

_____

_____

_____

_____

It is well
with my soul.

March

In the Field of Our Lives

Disregarding the impetuousness in which the month of March arrived, I've already started working in the garden again, little by little, as circumstances permit.

It is a jumble of dead leaves and putrid organic matter out here, and the garden resembles an abandoned field stripped down to its essence. Everywhere I look I see only muted hues of drab taupe, brutalized by the winter cold. But the sun is shining brightly today, and it is infusing the earth with warmth and joyfulness, making me squint in its brightness as it fills my heart with hope and a renewed awareness of God's presence.

Winter tends to do away with most of the glories found in the early summer garden, but even in the very midst of winter, there is always some goodness waiting to be revealed—a sacred wholesomeness that is just a tiny bit of what God has yet to reveal of Himself to His earthly children. Here and there, I can see—though almost invisible to the eye—tiny green buds on shrubs and trees.

Just as everything we create reveals our personality, our Creator left the mark of His character in all things He has made. He can be known through the works of His hands; His holy presence felt in each and every circumstance surrounding our life. However, just as the unaccustomed eye fails to find beauty in the apparent barrenness of the winter garden, the heart that does not know God would not be able to find Him.

When I'm in my garden on days like these, I don't have to see a single flower or leaf on my trees to know that they're still very much alive. Even though the landscape snoozes, life remains.

God is holy and present everywhere, always filling heaven and earth. He is always somewhere in the field of our lives, if we will only notice.

Talking to the Father

Lord, may You wash our souls with the salve of Your grace so that our eyes may see that we are never alone.

Immediate Attention

The soil is no longer wet, which means I can start removing fallen branches and debris. It also means I should start trimming plants before the old growth gets tangled up in the new growth.

The garden requires immediate attention, even before the growing season begins. If we wait to carry out the task of cleaning, we will wonder what to do to change it once it becomes an unsightly scene.

If perennials are left standing during the winter and are not pruned back as spring sets in, they will become unattractive and unruly. Plants that retain their leaves through the winter will present tattered foliage. Spring is the time to trim back and encourage new growth.

Still more important is the fact that some shrubby plants and woody perennials, such as the buddleia, or butterfly bush, Cestrum, and hummingbird flower, need to be cut back each spring because they only bloom on new branches. These plants are pruned in the spring to limit winter damage and encourage new growth.

> Do not be overcome by evil, but overcome evil with good.
> —Romans 12:21, ESV

> Spring-cleaning always inspires me to take an honest look
> at my life and determine which behaviors
> and habits are helping me grow closer to God.

I'm also preparing the garden to repel pests and disease by spraying deciduous trees and shrubs with fungicide and insecticide oils, pulling ugly weeds that spoil the beauty, and dividing and transplanting perennials to give them a better chance to survive.

All things considered, spring-cleaning is a prerequisite for a beautiful garden.

Spring-cleaning always inspires me to take an honest look at my life and determine which behaviors and habits are helping me grow closer to God, and which are hindering me from His precious light. It reminds me of Paul's advice to Christians: "I appeal to you therefore,

brothers, by the mercies of God, to present your bodies as a living sacrifice, holy and acceptable to God, which is your spiritual worship. Do not be conformed to this world, but be transformed by the renewal of your mind, that by testing you may discern what is the will of God, what is good and acceptable and perfect" (Romans 12:1, 2, ESV). Our mind, body, and soul need spring-cleaning just as much as our gardens.

Reflect

ᜃ How can you begin spring-cleaning your mind, body, and soul today?

_____

_____

_____

ᜃ What might be hindering you from getting closer to God?

_____

_____

_____

_____

"Be transformed
by the
renewal
of your mind."

Spring-Cleaning of the Soul

With spring comes a constant stream of chores and duties that the gardener must accomplish to prepare the garden for what's to come and help it mature into true beauty. There is debris to be removed from the garden's floor after the long winter, and the soil must be worked. We need to prune and cut dead stems and old stalks to make way for new shoots. This is the time to remove and compost any dead annual plants that remain from winter and prune plants that don't like to be pruned in the fall. The growth that will result after the pruning is too tender to survive the winter, and the dieback is often enough to kill the whole plant. Among the ones that need to be pruned now are the artemisia, the asters, the candytuft, and the lovely lilies.

Spring-cleaning also frees the garden of many leaf diseases and fungi that provide spores that can start a new epidemic. It is a terrific way to prevent plant diseases in the garden before the growing season gets started.

My work in the March garden reminds me of the garden of our soul. We need to clean it often to keep it alive and thriving. We need to take advantage of every opportunity to grow in holiness. There will always be influences that lead us away from God and a holy way of life, but just like our gardens, we can begin a new season of spiritual growth on our Christian journey toward God.

Spring gives us hope for rejuvenation in our own lives as well. It is also a time to renew the excitement and zest for life, and it encourages me to come clean with God. The confession of our sins, and the beauty of repentance, are like the spring-cleaning of the garden. They help remove from our lives the thoughts and actions that discourage our relationship with God.

> Rid yourselves of all the offenses you have committed, and get a new heart and a new spirit. Why will you die, people of Israel?
> —Ezekiel 18:31, NIV

God's Words

"Search me, O God, and know my heart: try me, and know my thoughts: And see if there be any wicked way in me, and lead me in the way everlasting" (Psalm 139:23, 24, KJV).

"Create in me a pure heart, O God, and renew a steadfast spirit within me" (Psalm 51:10, NIV).

March

Like Mourning Doves

The mourning doves are starting to engage in their courtship rituals. Their soothing song imbues the air with wonder and bonding sacraments—wings flapping, heads dipping in puffed up feathers, and guttural love songs.

My garden is a mourning dove refuge. They must like it here, I should think, and what a delightful situation this is. I am thankful. Thankful that they choose to hang around our snowy winter garden, rather than migrating, just so they can continue enticing my mornings with their soothing call.

I want to hold in the palm of my hands this weeping jewel that is the song of these gentle creatures, and retain it there if I only could. I want to make it part of my being, but instead, this song runs rampant in the hands of the wind. It flickers, mutates, and scurries to the ground like the pearls of a shattered necklace as the sun shimmers and twinkles through naked branches in cobalt hues stolen from the skies.

I lift my face up to heaven. . . . "Are You up there? Are You?"

I lift my face up to heaven, and reach with my arms out wide. "Are You up there? Are You?" In my heart. In my soul. In my very being, You are.

I, too, like the birds, have grown wings on my back. The scent of the wet earth and young leaves are part of this *rendezvous* of the soul. Hope is here! God walks again in my garden, an embodiment of grace and glory against the silent blue of the March sky.

Talking to the Father
Heavenly Father, how comforting and uplifting it is to know You. O Lord, You know every creature and every thing that breathes and You call it Yours. Let the song of my heart be safe in the hollow of Thy hand that I may be filled with the overflowing peace that runs from You—like a clean, rushing river. Have you wiped clean, O Lord, refreshed and revived in the pure joy of Your Holy Spirit. Please be with those who have hurt me, and heal our wounds. Help me forgive and forget, and move on like the birds of the sky, O Father.

> I know all the birds
> of the hills,
> and all that moves
> in the field is mine.
> —Psalms 50:11, ESV

Spring Knocking on My Door

I stand in the center of the garden under pristine sapphire skies. Sunshine on my face. Feet dancing in a circle of sunbeams. Is it easy to fly without moving? I have to wonder.

My spirit soars with feelings of awe and thankfulness as sunshine increases and the weather gets warmer. The blessings of spring knock on doors that have been locked for far too long. I'm rejuvenated in spirit and body.

Beautiful, generous light brings love and life into my little world.

Love. Love is in the air. It dances above the fields. It flutters about the garden and dashes in and out of it in the songs and courtships of birds. Love is expressed in the elaborate gowns of tulips and the crowned heads of sedum pushing through the ground after being woken up from their winter slumber. Love is everywhere. Like a soothing, blessed beverage, love enters your soul and fills it with joy.

Life. Life is stronger than death. Life, death, and, above all, this resurrection of the natural world in springtime resonates with power. Watching my garden, which is filled with perennials, bloom extravagantly in the summer and then die down in the fall, only to come to life again in the spring, is a reminder of God's promises. "I am the resurrection and the life. The one who believes in me will live, even though they die; and whoever lives by believing in me will never die" (John 11:25, 26, NIV).

My spring garden is a wellspring from which I draw inspiration. It is a place where life and death become a resurrection and a promise, a cycle of birth, development, maturity, death, and rebirth. A natural miracle performed in the name of divine love each year.

Talking to the Father
God, I am speechless. I can only stand before You in total humility and devotion. Bless the Lord, my soul, and bless God's holy name.

> Place me like a seal
> over your heart,
> like a seal
> on your arm;
> for love
> is as strong as death,
> its jealousy unyielding
> as the grave.
> It burns
> like blazing fire,
> like a mighty flame.
> —Song of Solomon 8:6, NIV

March

A Book of Promises

I'm exhausted. And there's not a single muscle in my body that does not ache. But it is good pain, tempered by the goodness of nature in response to a labor of love. The garden is getting ready.

Although temperatures are ever so fluctuating in these altitudes, I've already started living outside again. As it is, from evening to early morning we're still experiencing some cold weather, but the chilliness hanging over the trees and bare branches foretells a joyful story.

Springtime opens a book of promises to the attentive eye. A book filled with stories of delicious sunny days and balmy evenings, followed by cicada songs that fill starry nights. To stand in the middle of the early spring garden invites meditation. As we drink in this future beauty seen through the eye of faith, the mind is also inspired with glimpses of our future eternal home. Through faith in Jesus Christ, we look forward to the wonderful future God has in store for us.

This present world is broken and wearing out under the winter of sin and decay, but God has a glorious future prepared for those who love Him. Jesus said: "And if I go and prepare a place for you, I will come back and take you to be with me that you also may be where I am" (John 14:3, NIV).

Reflect

෴ Take a moment to consider how the spring-cleaning of your mind, body, and soul is progressing.

_____

_____

෴ Ask God to give you a glimpse of the home He is preparing for you today.

_____

_____

A World Without Flowers

Tulips are already popping up everywhere—a meager beginning for a heart that yearns for abundance. But I can't complain; this little garden of wonders is already looking glorious under the early spring skies.

Fully clad in dazzling hues of deep cobalt, the *Iris reticulata* is always the first ray of hope to burst in the garden. They are among the first signs of spring, popping up early and blooming quickly. They bring such joy to the gardener's eager heart.

God delights in revealing Himself in everything He made.

It is hard to imagine a world without flowers. They were meant to be a celebration of beauty and inspiration so that we may look to God through all that He created. In the life-death-regeneration cycle of the natural world, in the power of the seed and in the birds of the air, we can find indications that God is everywhere, in every season.

God isn't playing a game of hide-and-seek with humanity. He wants to be found, and that is why He delights in revealing Himself in everything He made.

God's Words

"For since the creation of the world God's invisible qualities—his eternal power and divine nature—have been clearly seen, being understood from what has been made, so that people are without excuse" (Romans 1:20, NIV).

> But will God indeed dwell on the earth? Behold, heaven and the highest heaven cannot contain you; how much less this house that I have built!
>
> —1 Kings 8:27, ESV

March

Sneaky as a Lioness

The month of March is as sneaky as a hunting lioness. When hunting, the lioness freezes and remains totally still, until finally she silently bursts from her cover and launches herself at her prey without warning.

In the Northern Hemisphere, the month of March teases us with warm temperatures and makes us believe that winter is finally over. But this is just to taunt us. There's always a final blow when you least expect it, and this morning it has brought in a whopping late winter storm that has sent us back below freezing. And the wind can be an aggressor of the soul. It howls and laughs at you, while you marvel at how the earth sits quietly and takes its assault.

The unpredictable and moody month of March reminds me of my own life sometimes. The wheel of faith hesitates, it gets stuck in a rut in the road. The eager early blooming flowers of all that is good and edifying to the soul are suddenly surprised by a late frost, and ice-edged daffodils hang their heads in sheepish dismay.

Thankfully, it will take only a few more weeks for the conclusion of winter. "Resist discouragement," the Holy Spirit within me whispers.

Talking to the Father
Lord, help me remember that discouragement is a choice. If I feel discouraged, it's because I've chosen to feel that way. Instead, help me trust in You with all my heart and not lean on feelings.

Reflect
ꙮ How can I keep my wheel of faith moving even when surprised by a late frost?

_____

ꙮ How can I practice leaning on God instead of my feelings?

_____

> Be strong,
> and let your heart
> take courage,
> all you who wait
> for the LORD!
> —Psalm 31:24, ESV

Our True Nature

Yesterday's storm brought ice back to the land. All bodies of water in the garden have frozen solid: birdbaths, fountains, and the small pond sitting on the edge of the west side of the garden.

As much as I try to like the month of March, my soul does not take well to its betrayals. March is a faker. It's hard to trust a month that breaks its promises. It changes directions and surprises us with its flashbacks to winter. It reminds me of common human nature.

> I can fully trust my little heart into Your loving hands.

How often do we put on appearances, only to act out in expression of our true nature? How often do we act in ways that revert to a previous life without Jesus? I think of Ananias and Sapphira, who presented a false image of themselves while acting out in dishonesty, hypocrisy, and pretense, more interested in appearances than true spirituality. To them Peter said, "You have not lied to man but to God" (Acts 5:4, ESV).

Even when we feel we can't trust a person or a month, we can always trust God.

Talking to the Father

How wonderful You are, Lord, that I can fully trust my little heart into Your loving hands. Thank You for not putting up an appearance of love. My heart rests in knowing that. I am in awe.

> I the LORD
> do not change.
> —Malachi 3:6, NIV

April

Spring makes its own statement,
so loud and clear that the gardener
seems to be only one of the instruments,
not the composer.

—Geoffrey B. Charlesworth

Graced by Rain

Last night, all night long, we were stirred from our sleep by the strong wind that is typically funneled into our valley by the mountain ranges that border it. It sounded unhappy. I heard it rummaging through the dry, brittle leaves in the garden, whipping trees and knocking on walls with restless sounds. Still, the windows of heaven kept shut, and rain wouldn't join its brother wind. Finally, this morning we were graced with the much-anticipated steady drizzle that my garden sorely needs.

My heart rejoices every time it rains. I love listening to the pitter-patter sound of raindrops striking the surface of the earth, creating the singing puddles, and rain droplets that drop like fat diamonds on leaves. Rain is grace; rain is the heavens descending onto the earth, for without rain there would be no life. And life is so full of beauty and wonder and glories stretched out upon our world by our gentle Creator.

I'm excited—delighting in the prospect of flowers after the rains. I rejoice in these moments. And it is the kind of enjoyment that directs my thoughts toward our Creator. Like the trees rooted in the ground rejoice in the rain, so rejoices the heart of the believer rooted in God's love.

This certainty allows me to truly enjoy each moment gifted to me. That's what Christians have done throughout the ages—sometimes in the most difficult situations—and that is what we are instructed to do daily.

Reflect
ᴥ How does God manifest His grace in my life?

_____

_____

God's Words
"Rejoice in the Lord always; again I will say, rejoice" (Philippians 4:4, ESV).

This is the day that the Lord has made; let us rejoice and be glad in it.
—Psalm 118:24, ESV

April

A Unique Song to Sing

We were seized by a rather unexpected winter storm all day yesterday. Blustery conditions and heavy fog held us prisoners in our own homes, we found ourselves wishing for the return of the sun.

The weather baffles me sometimes. It doesn't abide by schedules or calendars. Winter has a unique song to sing up here in the Northern Hemisphere, and it will not make a final departure until the last note has been well sounded.

I've been homebound and waiting rather impatiently for the glories that follow the final exodus of wintry weather. It may take yet a few more days for this to occur, but what delight has the beautiful sun of this morning brought to us. What joyful brightness—melting all gloominess into golden globules of warmth and happiness! My heart sings like a bird that has found its nest.

Come near to me, O Lord.

Oh, what luminous, exquisite loveliness the sun brings! I want to capture this riotous beauty and joyful sentiment in my heart, and I can only bow before my Lord in humble adoration and thankfulness. Isn't He the light of this world, the Light who shines in our darkness?

Talking to the Father

We have been imprisoned for far too long in this world of darkness, O Lord. We crave Your light. We crave Your nearness. To be whole again. To be able to live under the protection of shimmering wings. Darkness oppresses us. We're dying without Your wondrous, precious light. Come, so that we may become whole again.

An Ancient Desire

Spring is finally here! Something incomprehensible and marvelous has awakened in me: the need to plunge into the very existence of the garden.

What is it that impels our spirits to reconnect with God and respond to His call with deep delight when the world turns warm and beautiful in the early days of spring, when leaves and petals embrace the garden in an all-encompassing gesture of love and glory? This ancient desire, no doubt, must have been placed deep within our human DNA at the moment of our creation by God Himself.

> For behold,
> I create new heavens
> and a new earth, and the
> former things shall not
> be remembered
> or come into mind.
> —Isaiah 65:17, ESV

Everywhere they looked, there was God.

Coming in direct contact with nature has more than a physical benefit. It is therapeutic, it is healing, it connects us with God, and it allows us to relate to life on a fundamental level. Is it any wonder that God gifted Adam and Eve with a marvelous garden for a home as their wedding gift?

I can only imagine the amazement, the childlike joy, the expressions of delight in Adam and Eve! Their wonder and curiosity as they planted their first tree, the paramount joy as they started a new rosebush from a single stem and wandered through their natural home, discovering new glories each day. Everywhere they looked, there was God.

I like how the sweet cantor of Israel, David, refers to nature as he singles out the spectacle of heaven:

> The heavens declare the glory of God;
>   the skies proclaim the work of his hands.
> Day after day they pour forth speech;
>   night after night they reveal knowledge.
> They have no speech, they use no words;
>   no sound is heard from them.
> Yet their voice goes out into all the earth,

their words to the ends of the world.
In the heavens God has pitched a tent for the sun.
   It is like a bridegroom coming out of his chamber,
   like a champion rejoicing to run his course.
It rises at one end of the heavens
   and makes its circuit to the other;
   nothing is deprived of its warmth (Psalm 19:1–6, NIV).

"The skies proclaim the work of his hands."

No doubt about it: Adam and Eve must have spent their time in the Garden of Eden singing praises to their Creator as they worked the land and wandered around. Nature, as a part of God's revelation of Himself, reaffirms and testifies to His existence. This revelation doesn't cease. It occurs "day after day" and "night after night." We are constantly reminded of God's existence though the works of His hands. Hallelujah!

Talking to the Father

My heart is an empty vessel awaiting to be filled by Your Holy Spirit, O Lord. I stand in awe before You. I wait for You to descend onto me, to lift me up, to fill me with holy graces until my cup is full and running over. I am Your child, Father. Please scatter glimpses of Your presence along the paths I should walk today, so that my faith be reinforced in You.

Reflect

∾ What are my favorite ways to explore nature? And what do these activities teach me about the Creator?

_____

_____

_____

_____

Hunting for Little Treasures

The gentle sound of a wispy rain welcomed us to the new day this morning. In the garden, the music of trickling water from the fountains has started to serenade our days again, and the yellow western tanager has returned home.

Soon I will be discovering cups of twigs and grass in tree branches, and, hopefully, I will be seeing in them those diminutive eggs of glossy blue marked with brown spots.

I am excited. My heart is bursting with possibilities and dreams. I head out to the garden, oblivious to the weather, for I am on a mission: I am in pursuit of whatever gifts the rain might have left for me to discover out there. And I am never disappointed.

Every good gift and every perfect gift is from above, and cometh down from the Father of lights, with whom is no variableness, neither shadow of turning.
—James 1:17, KJV

Contemplate God's wondrous love.

The pansies that greet me from the northern beds are wearing liquid gems on their happy little faces. On each of their fingerlike petals, the Shasta daisies are exhibiting rings adorned in perfect jewels of spherical raindrops. Tulips have been dressed up in velvety apparel, their heads crowned with globular jewelry and trinkets of pure and dazzling luster. The entire garden is the ballroom where nature dances and renews itself under the blessings bestowed by rain.

I keep searching. I keep hunting for little treasures, for I know there are more. Then, as I stand looking around through wonder-filled eyes, I feel it— this joy, like a tangible delight leaping from the garden's floor, wet and supple, overflowing with promises.

It stretches out, this joy. It swells up and it spreads, leaving behind more blessings—a bird's indigo feather, a shiny pebble, and round silvery globules of raindrops hoarded in the jade cups of the sedum. They are gifts that I will later carry in my memories to cheer my soul as I contemplate God's wondrous love manifested through creation.

Reflect

❧ What gifts has God given to me in my corner of the world today?

_____

_____

_____

_____

❧ What new gifts can I praise God for today?

_____

_____

_____

_____

God's Words

"Let the heavens rejoice, let the earth be glad; let the sea resound, and all that is in it. Let the fields be jubilant, and everything in them; let all the trees of the forest sing for joy" (Psalm 96:11, 12, NIV).

NEST

Unexpected Blessings

While working in the garden today, I discovered two new peony bushes growing among the newly risen delphinium bed, over on the northern side of the garden. How and when were they planted there? I suppose this is the result of last fall's rearrangements, and my moving perennials around. A few peony tubers must had been left behind, and now they have reappeared.

I certainly wasn't expecting them there. Or to grow at all, as a matter of fact. But they have. And what a lovely surprise it has been!

I'm learning that as a garden matures, plants will reseed themselves. When the seeds ripen, their seedpods explode, sending seeds in all directions. Many plants are sown by seeds that have been eaten and excreted by birds. Other plants sprout from seeds transported by birds or other creatures. Trees can grow unexpectedly where squirrels have buried nuts and forgotten them.

> And if anyone gives even a cup of cold water to one of these little ones who is my disciple, truly I tell you, that person will certainly not lose their reward.
> —Matthew 10:42, NIV

"Love is from God."

These plants come into existence in a supernatural sort of way, don't you think? To me, they represent unexpected blessings. Small blessings, like little stars scattered all over the garden. I like to call them "heavenly surprises"— little gifts from my heavenly Father—of which I'm always in awe.

And these gifts are not limited to plants growing where you hadn't anticipated. They also show up in the unpretentious beauty of the wildflower. These may have absolutely nothing to do with your efforts but are simply gifted to you by the Master Gardener through whichever means He's chosen.

I wonder if this analogy also applies to people, to those who sometimes show up in our lives in unexpected, unconventional ways. I think of a family of immigrants in our church that my mother once took under her wing when we were growing up. She fed them, clothed them, and provided them with a temporary refuge until they could provide these things for themselves.

Sometimes God puts people in our path for a purpose. He calls us to be the vessels through which others can find their way to Him. I remember our

mother offering not only shelter and food to this family of strangers but also words of hope and encouragement. What if she hadn't been willing to take them in?

God's Words

"Beloved, let us love one another, for love is from God, and whoever loves has been born of God and knows God. Anyone who does not love does not know God, because God is love" (1 John 4:7, 8, ESV).

Reflect

❧ Who does God want me to pray for today? To reach out to?

_____

_____

_____

_____

❧ Create a list of your unexpected blessings.

_____

_____

_____

_____

_____

_____

> Heavenly surprises are little gifts from God.

Angels Live in My Garden

I honestly believe that angels live in my garden, perched on wings of prayers. I have learned to communicate with God face-to-face in the sanctuary of my garden. When weary or sad, when feeling joyful, ashamed, or fearful, I can always find in God an understanding Friend.

Between the river birch and the Callery pear there is a door leading to prayer. These two trees and the flowering crab apple are the main columns of this garden temple where I go to meet my Savior. Farther down, in that sacred corner where the heart-shaped leaves of the quaking aspen whisper soft, enchanting sounds as they tremble in light breezes, I find my pew and my hymnal.

The Japanese snowbell, its fragrant bell-shaped flowers tinted white in early summer and yellow in autumn, along with the smoke bush's gorgeous purple leaves and clusters of puff-of-smoke, are the decorations of the sanctuary. Pansies, peonies, and delphiniums serve as the deacons, deaconesses, and ministers of the garden.

Wounds heal, worries plummet, courage sparks, and faith increases, while the necessary tears are shed sans inhibition. Hidden away from the eye of the world in this natural environment, the confining harness of civilization drops off. Here I can always find Christ, my Refuge and Strength and ever-present Help in trouble.

Is it surprising that God planted a garden for humans to live in?

> *And my sleepy garden is slowly becoming a paradise again.*
> *Standing on the tip of the season it dances,*
> *it hovers over my heart like a butterfly.*
> *I see Your hand everywhere I look, O Lord.*
> *In the childhood of the new season,*
> *in the misty mornings of spring enchantment there You stand,*
> *a constant companion as bright as silence . . .*
> *deciphering the wordless prayers of my silent heart.*
> —Olga Valdivia

> I will walk among you and be your God, and you will be my people.
> —Leviticus 26:12, NIV

April

Like the Birds of the Air

It's bird season for sure. My little world is filled with the swish of feathers and morning songs. I am rewarding all the joy birds bring to the garden by providing for their needs. Birdbaths have been cleaned up, and every food station is brimming with all sorts of treats. Now bushy shrubs and trees have become homes and apartments for young couples and expectant mothers. Lately, even the Sally Holmes climbing rose growing gracefully by our master bedroom window has been embellished with the most creative of cradles for some wee ones.

Can you imagine being brought into this world on a bed of thorns and still being confident about your future? Birds, by all means, know how to trust. I love to watch them engage in courtship and bonding displays in earnest trust, to see them glide through the air in complicated patterns without the least of worries.

And who among us doesn't worry? Who doesn't get anxious or lose sleep over life's predicaments? In this sense, birds remind me of Jesus. They remind me of His teachings and how well He knows our human nature. Is it any wonder why the Son of God directs our thoughts to the birds of the air? "Look at the birds of the air; they do not sow or reap or store away in barns, and yet your heavenly Father feeds them. Are you not much more valuable than they?" (Matthew 6:26, NIV)

When Jesus walked on this earth, He emphatically instructed us to place all our cares upon His shoulders. One of His most frequent commands doesn't concern holiness or even love. "Fear not" is repeated throughout the Bible. There is approximately one "fear not" for every day of the year, as a matter of fact. Does this tell you something?

Why was Jesus so concerned about our peace of mind? In reality, what He is commanding is our trust. Peace of mind, holiness, and love are the natural consequences of a sincere trust in God.

Talking to the Father
Father, let us not forget that You command us to trust in You.

God's Classroom

The first year I started gardening, two of the rosebushes I'd planted the previous spring didn't make it through winter. I remember my disappointment and despondency. Hadn't I followed every piece of advice and every requirement for growing roses offered in the zillions of gardening books and magazines I read that year?

I knew that it would be difficult to protect roses during our winters. Even in some nurseries, covered plants were not immune from freezing. I was also informed that I should grow only plants that were hardy in our growing climate, those tough enough to make it through our winter months.

My only job was to add an adequate amount of mulch after the first ground freeze to insulate the roses from temperature fluctuations and not interfere with what they already knew to do: survive the winter.

I followed every possible rule, and certainly, most of my roses did survive. But there were still those unfortunate ones that didn't. What had happened? Was it my fault? Their fault?

A garden is God's classroom and a metaphor for life. Class is in session. Bibles open. Nature has seemingly unending lessons to teach us about life, the character of God, and what it means to be Christians of faith.

For now we see in a mirror dimly, but then face to face. Now I know in part; then I shall know fully, even as I have been fully known.
—1 Corinthians 13:12, ESV

Jesus dispels our doubts.

As I pondered on what could have happened to those roses that didn't make it that winter, while others did, my mind kept going back to the age-old conundrum of "Why does God allow bad things to happen to good people, while sinful people prosper?"

These uncertainties spurt into our minds when we see or hear about how pain and suffering touch people we know or care about. And our hearts are daily haunted by news of senseless violence and misfortune around our world.

Doubt creeps in because, recognizing our own finitude in all of it, we still can't answer these questions: Why is there suffering? Why do innocent people suffer harm, but guilty people often seem immune? Where is God when terrible things happen?

I don't think we will ever find the proper explanation for these questions, other than God's character is revealed most clearly not through our circumstances, but at the cross. At Calvary, Jesus dispels our doubts and shows us what God's true intentions are.

Perhaps we are not bound to win on this earth, but we are certainly bound to heaven and to our heavenly Father. And that's all that really matters.

I like this quote from Amy Carmichael: "Give Him time and, as surely as dawn follows night, there will break upon the heart a sense of certainty that cannot be shaken."

Reflect

∾ How does Calvary demonstrate God's love to you personally?

_____

_____

_____

_____

∾ Create a list of Bible verses that will strengthen your faith when doubts arise.

_____

_____

_____

_____

WELCOME

May

"Is the spring coming?" he said.
"What is it like?". . .
"It is the sun shining on the rain
and the rain falling on the sunshine."
—Frances Hodgson Burnett

May

A Taste of Heaven

My May garden bears no resemblance to my January garden! A taste of heaven is in the air. I can hear the sound of sacred feet approaching—a swish of wings over there, light streaming through blossomed branches, sweeping soft green grass. I am both Adam and Eve. God's spirit is flowing in graceful breezes, freely and boundlessly, over my dear little Eden.

To fancy being in the Garden of Eden on days like these is irresistible. But this is springtime after all! And dreamlike days are for imagining and dreaming and being joyful. It is that time of the year when the spirit is renovated and faith rekindled by the splendors of God's creation.

The earth has been awakened by golden sunshine. Tree branches are bursting with joyful buds, and tulips embellish the garden's floor in red and yellow buttons here and there. The garden is dressing up in supple greens and velvety splendor. The globes of Purple Sensation alliums never fail to delight. Chartreuse, emerald, jade, and shades of lime enter the picture as more perennials emerge. Fresh beauty hits my eyes wherever they look.

It never fails to amaze me—this disposition of the May garden. However sparse the landscape of the garden may look during the winter, all the planting beds overflow with life and color and joyful splendor as soon as the stronger sun of May appears.

I have so much I want to say, so much I'd like to share, but words escape me. I have only feelings of gratitude and a growing consciousness of the nearness of God's holy presence. A new light is shining upon the garden these days. This spring light is different from the light that shrouds the garden in other seasons. Everything I see and find here leads me to my Creator. I know with certainty I'm not alone in my garden.

Talking to the Father
Francis Thompson wrote,

> *O WORLD invisible, we view thee,*
> *O world intangible, we touch thee,*
> *O world unknowable, we know thee,*
> *Inapprehensible, we clutch thee!"*

Scent of Lilacs

The May wind is tossing the lilacs. This is the month when God breathes upon the garden and fills our days with clean, floral scents of honey pollen and jasmine-like freshness. But above all other scents, lilacs reign supreme!

Tiny purplish blossoms shaken from delicate stems scatter their fragrance in gentle waves over the garden throughout the day. With the pleasures of the scent of lilacs also comes the extraordinary effect of morning breezes arching flexible stems and the enigmatic singing of trees as gentle puffs of air rattle leaves and branches and the cozy houses of birds and other residents of my garden. And there, in the midst of it all, I find God. God molding and speaking into my reassurance-thirsty heart, singing His promises against the earlobes of my yearning soul. And I listen. And hear. And I also see the symbols of His love scattered throughout the garden's floor: birth, death, and resurrection—the archetypes and paradigms of the human race.

I think of what Adam and Eve must have felt after the consequences of sin marred their precious home. The sorrow. The hopelessness. Then I see them wiping away tears shed on a dream lost to the serpent. All glories lost. Every privilege removed . . . until they hear the sound of the Lord in the Garden in the cool of the day, remember the day they first met Him and felt the love in His great heart, and hear the words of promise (Genesis 3:15).

> Praise the LORD!
> praise God
> in His sanctuary;
> praise him
> in his mighty heavens!
> Praise him
> for his mighty deeds;
> praise Him
> according to his
> excellent greatness!
> —Psalm 150:1, 2, ESV

Talking to the Father
O Lord, before I step forth into my day, may my eyes be opened to Your eternal glories and my heart purified in Your endless love. This land is my cloak. But You are the Maker and Shelter of my wildflower soul.

Reflect:

❧ How does recognizing God as my shelter change the way I live each day?

_____

_____

May

A Creator-Creature Alliance

My heart
has heard you say,
"Come and talk
with me."
And my heart responds,
"LORD, I am coming."
—Psalm 27:8, NLT

Gardening has innumerable qualities that are beneficial to body, mind, and spirit. Gardening burns fat, builds muscles, and helps boost self-esteem and optimism. Gardening teaches us patience, shows us the beauty in imperfection, and allows us to let go of the wheel of stress. But gardening has more to it than just that. Its benefits go to deeper, more profound levels. It connects us to the Creator and to our human story. It is the Creator-creature alliance. I contemplate this while the sky above my head bears the cobalt color of the grape hyacinth on a spring's day.

I come to the garden absorbed in the pursuit of seeking God's presence, and as a gift I find that the *Delphinium belladonna* is in full bloom. Their prolific bright sky-blue flowers, gracefully enveloping each branching stem, convey the true nature of the color blue. They seem happy under the light streaming from the larger florets of the Pagan Purple Delphinium, sitting beside them in shimmering dark blues and deep purples.

Would I find God here? I ask myself. Oh, but I already have!

My soul rejoices in this knowledge. I rejoice in my surroundings. I rejoice in this amazing, all-powerful God by whose authority the earth awakens each spring in petals, colors, forms, scents, soil teeming with microscopic life, and creatures performing their individual functions. I give thanks. I bow before God, for again, I have found Him.

Reflect

❧ Is anything in my life preventing me from earnestly seeking God?

_____

_____

_____

_____

ꝏ What am I thankful for today?

_____

_____

_____

_____

Where do you
feel God's
presence the most?

God's Words

You, God, are my God,
   earnestly I seek you;
I thirst for you,
   my whole being longs for you,
in a dry and parched land
   where there is no water.
I have seen you in the sanctuary
   and beheld your power and your glory.
Because your love is better than life,
   my lips will glorify you.
I will praise you as long as I live,
   and in your name I will lift up my hands.
I will be fully satisfied as with the richest of foods;
   with singing lips my mouth will praise you
(Psalm 63:1–5, NIV).

May

Roses

Right before breakfast, as I'd usually do immediately after waking up each morning, I run to the tall windows in my kitchen to admire the happy rows of roses flanking my little world outside.

There are the luscious amethyst roses in sweet purple, and the vivid bright orange blooms of the trumpeter floribunda on the western wall, the lovely Royal Sunset in deep apricot shades creeping shyly up the wall. And then there are the beds of iceberg and Cinco de Mayo and Chicago Peace roses, all gloriously healthy and sturdy with perfect blooms and perfect leaves. All as expected. All of them there, like some loved children in the circle of a loving family.

I think of my dear roses and imagine how dumbfounded and heartbroken I would be if one morning I came out here to admire them and found some of them gone, snatched from the garden by some malevolent creature during the night hours.

Such disturbing thoughts get me pondering. Do I feel this upset by the thought of those who have stopped coming to church, those dear children of God who have left because, perhaps, they felt unloved, misunderstood, or mistreated?

Our church reports alarming membership losses each year, particularly among young adults. We cannot expect to keep every member in church. Nor can we think as our duty the job of bringing them *all* back. But I can certainly make sure those with whom I come in contact with every day, every week, do remain, by loving them and nurturing them.

Instead of belittling young adults with uncaring words and selfish deeds, let's make them want to stay home in the safety and warmth of a loving church.

God's Words

"A new command I give you: Love one another. As I have loved you, so you must love one another. By this everyone will know that you are my disciples, if you love one another" (John 13:34, 35, NIV).

> But God demonstrates his own love for us in this: While we were still sinners, Christ died for us.
>
> —Romans 5:8, NIV

Look At the Birds of the Sky

The minute I heard the elated chirps and whistles saturating the late spring morning, I knew a robin had just found my garden. Following the bird's loud, melodious chirrups, I searched the blossomed branches of the Callery pear tree with hopeful eyes, trying to locate my happy soloist. And there he was—with lovely peachy-orange feathers, ringing out his magnificent, sweet, and wild song.

I let my eyes wander over this scene for a while and listened. The bird's whistles and tweets sounded like precious promises being rung high above my head in notes that seemed to remind me: "Look at the birds They don't plant or harvest or store food in barns, for your heavenly Father feeds them. And aren't you far more valuable to him than they are?" (Matthew 6:26, NLT).

A simple wonder filled my heart. God's promises became flesh right that moment, breathing a new song of joy and praise into my heart. A God who can create and sustain such a delicate and precious creature must surely care about me.

> Look at the birds.
> They don't plant
> or harvest
> or store food in barns,
> for your heavenly Father
> feeds them.
> And aren't you far more
> valuable to him
> than they are?
> —Matthew 6:26, NLT

> A God who can create and sustain such a
> delicate and precious creature must surely care about me.

How I wished then to be able to hold this magnificent living creature of the air in my open hands and retain his songs of trust and conviction forever in my heart. I wanted him forever perched in my suburban garden, but instead, as if attempting to preserve my sense of wonder, the bird suddenly stopped singing, and with an almost soundless swiftness of wings, he left the branch and flew away.

We could surmise that Jesus was only trying to point to the relatively higher worth of human beings versus birds, but He was actually trying to show us that worrying is really a lack of trust in God. I like to think that perhaps Jesus was also trying to bring our attention to the practice of focusing on this moment. You see, nothing is worth more than this day. The present is a precious gift from God that too often is taken for granted. Yesterday is history, tomorrow is a mystery, we have only today. And that's what Jesus wants us to see.

We have the tendency to take things for granted, even things we have come to depend on, such as our homes or the food we eat. Because we see some things so often, we notice them less and less. God's beautiful creation—such as birds, flowers, the rainbow after a rainy day—are often unnoticed or unappreciated. The many blessings that surround us, including our loved ones, become invisible to us.

We ask God for miracles. Like Moses, we ask to see His face. But I have to ponder if the wonder and yearning of our hearts would remain the same if even seeing His face became a routine. We can't afford to take for granted God's glories all around us. We should live each moment mindfully, enjoying the hours we are gifted on this earth by consciously paying close attention to our surroundings and to those with whom we share this road called life.

Reflect

ꙮ How is God revealing His glory to me?

_____

_____

_____

ꙮ In what areas of my life do I need to be intentional about living in a
more mindful manner?

_____

_____

_____

God's Words

Oh, give me the meadow flowers, and give me the waking up to the first flock of robins in the garden. Give me the little things that bestow joy and peace to my heart. For "I will be fully satisfied as with the richest of foods; with singing lips my mouth will praise you" (Psalm 63:5, NIV).

Perfect Glory

The minute I walked into my beloved garden this morning, my spirit was lifted. And how could it not be? Some of the rosebushes are now in full bloom. Perfect roses. Perfect petals. Perfect glory! Anywhere my eyes rested, I'd see roses wearing the softest palettes of rainbows and gala gowns in shades of pink, reds, and yellows. I can almost hear them sing: "Clap, sing to the Creator of all things, for His mercies are everlasting."

With the roses, as faithful companions and cohorts at this grand ball, there are the blue flag irises, the shooting stars, and bleeding hearts—all in full bloom. Wispy columbines resembling diminutives ballerinas are here too, and with them have come all the lush ornamental grasses, embellishing some of the beds.

This riot of undisciplined colors, scents, and forms greets all my senses and humbles my heart before my Creator. I cannot but let my voice unite with that of nature in praises of adoration to God, in whom I trust.

As I sang and praised God in the beauty all around me, the garden seemed to be telling me: "Grasp these demonstrations of love and truthfulness suspended in pure, shining colors. Take them in the circle of your hands, take them in your brain and in your heart. Then go out into the world and scatter these heavenly jewels all around."

What a magnificent lesson the garden teaches me this morning—one of humbleness and adoration and a determination to see the lost find their way to this awesome Creator, who is also the Savior of this world.

Ascribe to the LORD the glory due his name; worship the LORD in the splendor of his holiness.
—Psalm 29:2, NIV

Talking to the Father

Father, help me share the greatness of this news with whomever I come in contact with today. Help me find ways to worship You in the splendor of Your holiness.

May

Teach Me Your Ways

The late May evenings have stories to tell. They impel you to go out and look for glimpses of God upon the hours of twilight. Thus, I go out and wait there for God to show Himself.

As night shadows come and melt away the last drop of goldenrod sunshine, I listen to the array of voices with which the natural world surrounds itself before nightfall. The murmur and tremors of small creatures; the intriguing songs of night birds, crickets, and spring peepers; the coos, screeches, and chatters of the night all beckon me. I am made aware of God's presence in a profound, humbling way.

Although enough glimpses of God's glories had been revealed, my yearning heart waits for more. It hungers for a deeper and more fulfilling encounter with its Redeemer. It yearns for a personal experience; it wants Him to fill its cup to overflowing.

It isn't a presumption or a sin to desire to know God's glory. Moses desired to know God's glory. He petitioned God, "If you are pleased with me, teach me your ways so I may know you and continue to find favor with you" (Exodus 33:13, NIV).

God's response to Moses humbles me and fills my heart with wonder and hope: "And the LORD said to Moses, 'I will do the very thing you have asked, because I am pleased with you and I know you by name' " (Exodus 33:17, NIV). In his quest to know the Omnipotent God, Moses learned that God knew him by name. This is a God I want to know.

> Blessed are those whose help is the God of Jacob,
>   whose hope is in the LORD their God.
> He is the Maker of heaven and earth,
>   the sea, and everything in them—
>   he remains faithful forever (Psalm 146:5, 6, NIV).

Now therefore,
I pray thee,
if I have found grace
in thy sight,
shew me now thy way,
that I may know thee,
that I may find grace
in thy sight:
and consider that this
nation is thy people.
—Exodus 33:13, KJV

Beauty and Songs

God opened His hands, and the air was filled with beauty and songs. Songs in the wings of the mourning dove, and songs in the yellow throat of the western tanager. Music in the leaves and branches of trees as they bend and lean and swing to morning breezes.

The natural world sings in many voices—all individually, and all together. Like in a symphony, each little winged creature, each organism, each insect—every living thing—delivers a unique message, its own unambiguous resonance: a jingle, a swish, a clatter, a song.

And how wonderful and thoughtful of God to have placed the enchanting, soothing coos in the throats of mourning doves and the high twittering in the blackbird's music box. With its *conk-la-ree*, *conk-la-ree*, the blackbird introduces me to the spring mornings.

How grand are the works of God's hands! I marvel at birds and their abilities to imbue the earth with joy in their varying actions and colors and songs. I'm so thankful our little feathered friends were in the loving, imaginative mind of God at the time of Creation. Their existence, without doubt, is an additional affirmation of God's divine nature and love for us.

> For since the creation of the world God's invisible qualities—his eternal power and divine nature—have been clearly seen, being understood from what has been made, so that people are without excuse.
> —Romans 1:20, NIV

God's Words
"I know all the birds of the hills, and all that moves in the field is mine" (Psalm 50:11, ESV).

May

In Intimacy With God

Something wonderful is happening in me. I can't explain the mechanisms of how it works or what to call it, but I'm sure it must have something to do with the amount of time I'm spending in the garden in intimacy with God. It is obviously the quiet workings of the Holy Spirit in me, infusing my tired, old self with new life and hope through a renewed love relationship between Creator and creature, my Savior and me.

It also has to do with the physical and mental benefits gardening provides. Every day, for weeks now, I have been outside working with the earth. I've been breathing in the pure air from my own paradise, under heartwarming sunshine. And I've been wild with joy among the roses and birdsong, wild in love with Jesus. Have I said this enough? Oh, but it bears repeating!

Working in partnership with the Master Gardener has opened new perspectives in life. It has unfastened the door of faith and widened the path to Christ. It has strengthened my trust in God and His promises and given me the certainty of a better future.

True joy is a fruit of the Spirit. And because it can come only from God, it is a special gift that only the true believer is allowed to have.

God's Words

"When you believed, you were marked in him with a seal, the promised Holy Spirit, who is a deposit guaranteeing our inheritance until the redemption of those who are God's possession—to the praise of his glory" (Ephesians 1:13, 14, NIV).

> You have enlarged
> the nation
> and increased
> their joy;
> they rejoice
> before you
> as people rejoice
> at the harvest,
> as warriors rejoice
> when dividing
> the plunder.
> —Isaiah 9:3, NIV

WELCOME

June

Green was the silence, wet was the light,
the month of June trembled like a butterfly.
—Pablo Neruda

June

This Mingling of Roots

Two New Dawn climbing roses were gifted to me this past Mother's Day. One was planted at the feet of the newly built arbor in the center of the garden. The other, outside one of my kitchen windows overlooking the entrance of the garden; and what precious joy these treasures bring into my life! I can already envision curtains of soft pink petals rustling in warm afternoon breezes.

The gladiolas are already showing their happy heads, tinted in vibrant reds and mellow yellows, as are the agapanthuses. In one of the flower beds, French Lace roses salute the morning in the shyest palette of pinks. Orange, yellow, and magenta flowers grow happily on the same stems of the snapdragons, and over by the eastern wall, the salvia paints my view with a magical purplish light.

I love this mixture of many layers of vegetation and grass all over the garden—shiny emerald and silvery greens amid splashes of purples, oranges, blues, and pinks. This intermingling of many shades, forms, scents, and textures is what makes my garden unique.

> Maybe, just maybe, this mingling of roots is a call to kinship, a place where diversity and acceptance hold hands.

Sometimes I wonder if this harmony extends beneath the earth's surface as well. Is there also a peaceful neighborhood of sorts underground, where a diversity of roots—all different from one another, all unique and distinct in their own right—coexist, like loving siblings in a large family?

Maybe, just maybe, this mingling of roots is a call to kinship, a place where diversity and acceptance hold hands. A place where the strong roots of impressive trees don't look down at the hair-thin roots of young plants, or where the strong, healthy roots of roses don't deride other roots for producing less attractive flowers, and where all inhabitants down under feel safe and free to be themselves and grow in unity under the law of respect and love.

And maybe there is a message here for God's church. We Christians can certainly look good on the outside. We can pretend kindness. We can be all smiles. We can make ourselves look good in the eyes of others. As the body of Christ, we can even give the impression of a triumphant church. But what's inside of us, hidden from the obvious, is what truly matters. How we treat others, and how we make others feel, is what God sees.

He has given us clear instructions on how to treat others, and what He says in His Word concerning this subject is just as binding and necessary as any other important lesson there given. We need to examine ourselves to see if we are treating others with a true Christian heart.

Ask God to help you show His love.

Reflect

ॐ How does God want me to appreciate and encourage others today?

_____

_____

_____

ॐ Do an attitude check: Am I living in a kind and compassionate manner toward others?

_____

_____

_____

God's Words

"Be kind and compassionate to one another, forgiving each other, just as in Christ God forgave you. Follow God's example, therefore, as dearly loved children and walk in the way of love, just as Christ loved us and gave himself up for us as a fragrant offering and sacrifice to God" (Ephesians 4:32–5:2, NIV).

June

In the Beginning

"In the beginning God . . ." Just four words. Simple words. Powerful words. They encompass life itself in its most profound sense. They take us to the mere beginning of all beginnings. And God in the beginning is also God in the end.

Today, that message is particularly clear through the wonderful display of nature right under my feet. The ground is covered in tiny puffs of brilliant fuchsia blooms! A delightful ground-hugging carpet formed by the ice plant that faithfully blooms season after season. And if you look over to your right, the Hemerocallis are also in bloom. *Lirio de San Juan, azucenas amarillas, azucena turca, lirio de la mañana.* I love their variety and their foreign names!

> Today, the summer sky reminds me
> of God's eternity in the softest of blues.

And the sky? Today, the summer sky reminds me of God's eternity in the softest of blues. Nature's choirs praise its Creator in an outstanding inter-action of voices and sounds and signals. Frog croaks, bird chirps, honeybee waggle dances—the panoply of ways animals transmit information to one another and to other denizens of the animal kingdom, all are manifestations of God and His remarkable design skills.

Whoever wants to hear, let them hear. And whoever wants to see, let them see. Let the heavens and the earth believe! God in the beginning is also God in the end: God at the end of the journey, God at the end of all hopes, God beyond our human finitude. And hasn't He made known from the be-ginning what is still to come? His purpose will stand. He will do all that He has said (see Isaiah 46:10).

In the beginning
God . . .
—Genesis 1:1, NIV

Silly, Wild Moments

There's a storm taking shape on the eastern sky. From where I stand, in the middle of the garden, I can see low, dark clouds, devoid of light and soaring on wings of air atop the mountains. They resemble prehistoric birds swiftly traveling this vastness of a dull sky as winds push them forward, quickly shifting their fleeting forms.

Wind. Wind is a mystery to me. Wind whips things around, it splits trees and blows roofs off houses as it pleases. I find strong winds unnerving. Nevertheless, there is something powerful and inexplicably exhilarating in the nature of wind that attracts me to it.

I harbor the adventurous spirit of a storm chaser inside me—riding the air in flowing, long skirts that swirl atop magical-looking clouds. And thus, although all my senses tell me I should go inside, I remain in the garden a little longer.

The rain-laden sky opens its murky mouth mockingly, and I hear winds howling directly overhead. Objects and things, wrapped in a wild swirl of rose petals, are thrown by the wind in all directions now. I look up to the sky and cannot see a thing. Dusty wind-glare obscures my vision. Yet my mind remains shut to the voice of my now frightened heart.

I dance and leap, delighted in my surroundings, until finally the first big, round splashes of raindrops hit the garden's floor in a sudden rush. I'm still ridiculously laughing my lungs out as the wind and rain tickle me happy.

A silly, wild moment. Fortunately, this is just a summer storm with minimal damage. I can't even begin to understand the horrific forces of swirling masses of air in a serious storm. Winds sometimes approach 200 miles per hour. Finding refuge from one of those storms is a matter of life and death.

When life's storms hit, I know where to run. The prophet Isaiah was well acquainted with that unfathomable shelter that is Christ, and he went to find refuge there often. I like how the prophet puts it: "[He] will be a shelter and shade from the heat of the day, and a refuge and hiding place from the storm and rain" (Isaiah 4:6, NIV).

> He caused an east wind to blow in the heaven: and by his power he brought in the south wind.
> —Psalm 78:26, KJV

June

In Humble Admiration

I could not have awakened to a more delightful day—the sound of rain all over my pillow; cerulean skies taunting me to dream beyond my circumstances. I want to be fully immersed in this atmosphere of light summer rain and scents forever. I run to my window and open it wide. In the garden, rain showers mingle with petals, and the air is thick with the scent of June: an amalgamation of blossoms and wet soil.

What a beautiful, amazing world God has given us!

The scent of rain plays garden games with the dense clusters of the late blooming Korean lilacs and the snowball viburnum's white flowers. And raindrops sparkle on the folds of roses. They twinkle on and off, as if wanting to call my attention. I want to believe they are fallen stars sleeping on green leaves.

What a beautiful, amazing world God has given us! I cannot but bow in humble admiration before God, the Creator who extended the heavens like silky sheets of blues and who gives showers of rain to all people.

Drip down, O heavens, from above,
And let the clouds pour down righteousness;
Let the earth open up and salvation bear fruit,
And righteousness spring up with it.
I, the Lord, have created it (Isaiah 45:8, NASB).

Imitating the Harmony of the Garden

My garden is a puzzle of forms, colors, and scents these days. It's a house outside the house where flowers, shrubs, and trees make cozy companions with one another and shade one another's feet. Every plant and shrub here embrace one another, free to grow where they are planted and always conferring the best of themselves.

No space is empty here. No color purposely paired. No bush or flower holds a higher value among the others. All are different. All are unique. All are vital in the unity that gives my little patch its welcoming and free personality.

Sameness without adequate difference can only lead to a boring whole. But harmony out of diversity produces a lively garden. The same can be applied to so many other areas in life.

My garden reminds me of what fellowship among Christians should be. A diversity of individuals (races, nationalities, genders, ages) growing together under the grace of God, encouraging one another, building up one another in every circumstance. Free to do good, to bring beauty to the world through faith imbued with godly attitudes. Free to pass the joy of knowing Christ to those around them in humility and love.

Whenever I hear about relationships among church members turned sour, I just have to wonder about how God, who created such perfect harmony in the natural world, must feel about it. Sometimes, relationship troubles in the church can lead to a congregation split into factions. I want to imitate the harmony of my garden in my relationship with fellow church members and walk in love, as Christ also loves us.

> Dear friends, let us love one another, for love comes from God. Everyone who loves has been born of God and knows God. Whoever does not love does not know God, because God is love.
> —1 John 4:7, 8, NIV

God's Words

"Let all bitterness, wrath, anger, clamor, and evil speaking be put away from you, with all malice. And be kind to one another, tenderhearted, forgiving one another, even as God in Christ forgave you" (Ephesians 4:31, 32, NKJV).

June

Ruffled Skirts

The Royal Amethyst rosebush is blooming profusely, and so are the bushes of the Chicago Peace on the south-facing wall. An old-time favorite, the Full Sail hybrid tea rose is waking up to the new morning with young florets protected in a petal-tight cocoon of the palest hues: the white rose—symbol of saints, purity, and happy brides.

I cut a large bucketful of roses this morning and brought it in to spread the tender posies around the house: Roses in the bedroom. Roses on the kitchen table. Roses on windowsills and bathroom vanities.

The layers of sumptuous ruffled skirts of petals, the palest of pinks, the lusciousness of purples, and the purity of whites. The soft, silky feel that evokes tenderness, the fragrant scent that brings refreshment. There's no question that above all flowers, roses bring forth the dazzling beauty of creation like none other.

Roses also prompt me to think of the inventiveness and humor of our Creator, who later would place qualities of the rose in the perfect woman He created.

George William Curtis wrote that "the fragrance always stays in the hand that gives the rose." Let the fragrance of our spirit sweeten the air of those around us with kindness, love, joy, peace, patience, goodness, faithfulness, gentleness, and self-control. That distinctive, sweet smell is the Spirit of God growing His fruit in the lives of believers.

God's Words
"She opens her mouth with wisdom, and the teaching of kindness is on her tongue" (Proverbs 31:26, ESV).

Like the Flowers of the Field

Hours, days, time passing by—dissolving into nothingness before the astounded eye. Time stimulates the flowers of the field, withering and falling from one day to the next, as so do we. We blossom like wildflowers, and our glory withers and disappears before we even realize the speed in which time imprisons us and takes us with it.

And here I am, astounded too. But like a bird, my heart soars heavenward with hymns to the Great I AM. For even if my body shall decay like the grass of the fields, and the beauty of my youth turn out like the flowers that fade and die, I shall still stand before my God one day.

> But like a bird, my heart soars heavenward
> with hymns to the Great I AM.

The realization of the apparent senselessness and finitude of life can overwhelm and debilitate even the strongest. David, in all his bravery, power, and authority, wrestled with this: "The life of mortals is like grass, they flourish like a flower of the field; the wind blows over it and it is gone, and its place remembers it no more" (Psalm 103:15, 16, NIV).

Every creature is as short-lived as grass, but faithful is the One who promised: "I am the resurrection and the life. The one who believes in me will live, even though they die; and whoever lives by believing in me will never die" (John 11:25, 26, NIV).

> The life of mortals
> is like grass,
> they flourish like
> a flower of the field.
> —Psalm 103:15, NIV

June

A Return to Paradise

Behold, I am with you
and will keep you
wherever you go,
and will bring you back
to this land.
For I will not leave you
until I have done what
I have promised you.
—Genesis 28:15, ESV

Whenever I'm out here in the garden, I am reminded that the deepest yearning of my heart is a return to Paradise. It never fails. Something invariably stirs in me a sense of belonging somewhere other than on this earth; it is a knowledge, a memory that transcends time, all of which tells me that, somehow, my soul is connected to Eve's Paradise.

My yearning for Paradise is a form of homesickness, a longing for my true home in heaven. It is not uncharacteristic for the true Christian to experience this spiritual hunger. Within us resides a seed sown in Eden—this aching for a place where humanity and nature can coexist in perfect harmony and where the alliance between creature and Creator can be rightfully restored, reaffirmed, and renewed forevermore.

We are connected to Eve and her memories of Eden by way of umbilical cord to umbilical cord since her creation. This hunger that we carry in our hearts, this yearning for the unspoiled life of humanity's beginning—a life unmarred and unending—was put in us by God Himself. He designed us to desire what He intended for us at Creation. We are simply responding to the invitation God has placed within us.

Reflect

❧ What is making me homesick for Paradise today?

_____

_____

❧ As I consider the hope of reunion with God in Paradise, what am I especially thankful for?

_____

_____

God's Words

"He will wipe away every tear from their eyes, and death shall be no more, neither shall there be mourning, nor crying, nor pain anymore, for the former things have passed away" (Revelation 21:4, ESV).

Are you homesick for heaven?

WELCOME

July

Let us dance in the sun,
wearing wild flowers in our hair.
—Susan Polis Schutz

July

A Dance Under the Sun

On warm afternoons, when the sun hits full over the boundaries of my florid garden, the smallest single-wing turquoise hummingbirds congregate in flittering jamborees, sipping nectar with straw-shaped tongues as they dance, suspended by the wind.

I love to watch these diminutive feathered creatures who, without a proper introduction, show up in my garden and engage in a glorious flickering of wings. I catch them fluttering and flapping their wee wings in the sunshine as I stand close by—arms out wide in invitation while I wait and hope in sheer anticipation that perhaps one of them would want to land on my fingertips.

My heart laughs with joy watching them. And somewhere in the distance, angels watch and smile too. Heaven—oh, what it will be! My heaven-loving heart yearns for a thaw, hoping for a ribbon of holiness to sneak its way into this sin-infected world and wrap every good thing in its warmth with the iridescent bow of eternal life.

> But in keeping with his promise we are looking forward to a new heaven and a new earth, where righteousness dwells.
> —2 Peter 3:13, NIV

Talking to the Father

We are not forsaken. My heart sings one pure, long note; it beats with heavenly rhythm.

> *The LORD will surely comfort Zion*
> *and will look with compassion on all her ruins;*
> *he will make her deserts like Eden,*
> *her wastelands like the garden of the LORD.*
> *Joy and gladness will be found in her,*
> *thanksgiving and the sound of singing*
> (Isaiah 51:3, NIV).

July

Ask the Animals

It's been raining oceans around here, and the garden has come alive with myriads of emerald greens and bright jewels—flowers and raindrops. It is almost unreal to look at this brilliance and realize that only yesterday my little world was bare and thin.

I've been living out here as much as the weather permits. I sit under the trees and try to drink in every detail surrounding me: the way nature seems to hug me; the wholesome warmth caressing my skin; the cloudless, dazzling blue sky greeting me again and again; swishing sounds behind my back; wee animals scurrying through the foliage; the rustle of thrashers foraging for food on the garden's floor; the twits and busyness of several other birds; the song of insects in sultry air.

> Ask the beasts, and let them teach you;
> and the birds of the heavens, and let them tell you.

If I close my eyes, I can imagine I'm listening to the sounds of the jungle. I can hear the monkeys high in the treetops collecting bits of branches, whooping and shrieking up in the billowy surface of the canopy. A screech, a howl. Bushes around me shaking and rustling. Until God's voice breaks in and silences all other voices:

> "Where were you when I laid the foundation of the earth?
> Tell Me, if you have understanding,
> Who set its measurements? Since you know.
> Or who stretched the line on it?
> On what were its bases sunk? . . .
> Have you ever in your life commanded the morning,
> And caused the dawn to know its place,
> That it might take hold of the ends of the earth, . . .
> Have you understood the expanse of the earth?

Tell Me, if you know all this.
Where is the way to the dwelling of light?
And darkness, where is its place, . . .
Who prepares for the raven its nourishment
When its young cry to God
And wander about without food?"
(Job 38:4–41, NASB).

"But now ask the beasts, and let them teach you; And the birds of the heavens, and let them tell you" (Job 12:7, NASB).

Talking to the Father

I am but an insignificant speck of dust before Your majesty, O Lord. Finding joy in Your creation comforts me. What other god can do the things that You do? In You only my heart finds rest.

Reflect

∾ List your favorite animals. How does God speak to you through their life and personality?

_____

_____

_____

_____

∾ How does the animal kingdom display God's glory to you?

_____

_____

_____

_____

July

"Higher Places"

> He had a dream in which he saw a stairway resting on the earth, with its top reaching to heaven, and the angels of God were ascending and descending on it.
> —Genesis 28:12, NIV

I have a Father who lives in higher places . . .
Isn't that what the Book of the Ages assures us?
"Our Father who art in heaven . . . "
So you think you got it all figured out . . .
You have found the ultimate meaning: love and purpose;
No disruption, troubles are under control, and yet . . .
There's something missing inside you.
I know . . . I, too, am chasing shadows of myself.
And the grandfather clock is ticking
tick-tock-tick-tock-tick-tock.
The world is spinning, spinning 'round and 'round, inside and outside.
When your heart is overwhelmed within you,
where do you seek refuge?
I climb up the heavenly stairs . . .
to "higher places"—
to my Father's house.
    —Olga Valdivia

Talking to the Father
Heavenly Father, thank You for providing a way for us to get to You.

Be Always on Watch

One would be tempted to think that hot July is the slowest period in the garden. But nothing could be further from the truth. In reality, a quiet time for the gardener it is not.

July is pruning time for hydrangeas, deciduous fruit trees, shrubs, and other plants that need shaping. It is also time to fertilize and renew old layers of mulch. Roses, bedding plants, and perennials need to be deadheaded to keep them looking tidy and encourage further flowering.

As flowers and plants grow rampant in the heat of summer, some of them need to be staked. Old ties need to be replaced, as they can do a lot of damage to plant tissue if they become too tight. By now, some of the ornamental grasses have become brown. The large zinnias are looking scraggy in their flower beds, and the conscious gardener must attend to all of this if they want their garden to remain in pristine condition.

Be always on the watch,
and pray that you may
be able to escape all
that is about to happen,
and that you may be
able to stand before the
Son of Man.
—Luke 21:36, NIV

> When we leave the garden of our heart unkempt
> and let the weeds of hatred, anger, bitterness,
> and discontent grow rampant,
> it is possible to lose our way and become lost.

There are other duties in the garden besides tending flowers that need be accomplished as well. The uneven and worn-out garden paths need fixing, the lawn mower and Weed eater usually require servicing, and all pruners, loppers, and hedge cutters have lost their sharpness.

July is indeed a busy month in the garden. One mustn't remain idle. If you decide that the hot months of summer are to be taken easy, things can get out of hand very quickly.

Guard
your heart.

The month of July seems to be telling me, "Be on your guard." I'm reminded that, spiritually speaking, we must not think that once we are saved we are saved forever. When we leave the garden of our heart unkempt and let the weeds of hatred, anger, bitterness, and discontent grow rampant, it is possible to lose our way and become lost.

It is no wonder God reminds us: "Be on your guard; stand firm in the faith; be courageous; be strong" (1 Corinthians 16:13, NIV).

Reflect

∾ How can I actively "be on my guard" today?

_____

_____

_____

_____

∾ What, if anything, is preventing me from watching and staying alert?

_____

_____

_____

_____

_____

My Hope Is in You

The heat of summer has drained the garden of freshness and energy. Future prospects are dimmed. But perhaps things aren't as bad as I see them; for negative thoughts may be dominating my thinking. I decide to write:

> I'm walking—inside out.
> Around me, darkness.
> In search of the Light that would make me whole, I walk;
> The radiance that would enlighten me, I seek;
> Sheathed in utter shielding.
> Supreme love, incomprehensible to the human mind,
> Yet propitiously perceptible to the heart of the seeker.
> Faith is neither logical nor illogical, but rather miraculous.
> Buried within me burns a flame.
> It is my choice as to whether I will see through the eyes of faith
> Or disbelief.
> Buried in Thy blood, Thy greatness I see.
> In Your death abides *my* death—victorious in Thy resurrection.
> Rediscovered.
> Reclaimed.
> Redeemed.

Life is rarely as bad as we see it. It is wise to pause from time to time and contemplate the blessings with which God has clothed us. Count your blessings. You will be encouraged.

God's Words

"Bless the LORD, O my soul, and forget not all his benefits" (Psalm 103:2, ESV).

And now, O LORD, for what do I wait? My hope is in you.
—Psalm 39:7, ESV

July

Summer Evenings

We are surrounded—delimited by zillions of diminutive bodies and creatures of the atmosphere embroidering the air in intricate winged designs: insects.

It is that time of the year when bugs and insects take over gardens and woody areas, creating the late summer buzz that some of us hate and some adore. I love it. Love that high-pitched hum of cicadas at 2:00 P.M. and at those precious hours right before dusk.

But here, cicadas are nonexistent. Here in my garden, it is a flurry of whiteflies and whatnots. These little bugs are often undetected until someone brushes by a plant. Then, what seems like a white cloud flies up. Their minuscule bodies meander through the early evening air, zigzagging invisible paths. When touched by the soft golden light of dusk, they become visible, almost glowing in midair, enticing you to join them, to dance with them under this wonderful, glorious light of late summer.

And then there are the sparkling, dew-tinged designs of silk—spider webs that seem to twinkle and dance from the rooftops down to the garden's floor when agitated by the last drop of goldenrod light.

> Certainly, nothing is everlasting in this world,
> but we can rest assured in God's promises.

It's the enchantment of summer evenings in the garden. And I am here—clinging to the miracle of the moment, not wanting to let go of it, as if by doing so I could retain summer eternally. But alas, I must say goodbye to the month's last wave of enchantment as it disintegrates along the flower beds in my garden with each ticktock of the clock.

Summer lingers in many a heart. Summers here are a fleeting, dear thing, and soon we must bid our last farewell to warm, sunny days, until the wheel of time brings it back to us for yet another moment in the calendar of our history. Hopefully, we'll be here to receive it and welcome it in our lives once again.

Certainly, nothing is everlasting in this world, but we can rest assured in God's promises. They are our only sure anchor. "Through these he has given us his very great and precious promises, so that through them you may participate in the divine nature, having escaped the corruption in the world caused by evil desires" (2 Peter 1:4, NIV).

God has promised us everlasting life. This is the future of the redeemed. It is our final reward and glory.

As Violette Leduc writes in Mad in Pursuit, "I walk without flinching through the burning cathedral of the summer. My bank of wild grass is majestic and full of music. It is a fire that solitude presses against my lips."

Rest in God's promises.

Reflect

❧ In what ways is God revealing His promises to me?

_____

_____

_____

_____

❧ What am I thankful for today?

_____

_____

_____

_____

August

The first week of August hangs at the very top of summer, …
like the highest seat of a Ferris wheel when it pauses in its turning.
The weeks that come before are only a climb from balmy spring,
and those that follow a drop to the chill of autumn,
but the first week of August is motionless and hot.
It is curiously silent, too, with blank white dawns
and glaring noons, and sunsets smeared with too much color.

—Natalie Babbitt

The Exultant Hours of Summer

Today a dense mist hangs in the atmosphere from the waking of morning to midday. It's the heat, condensed as it is into a melting fog. Heat liquefying my thoughts. Heat tying my dreams into a contemptible knot of insects, heavy perspiration, and some poisonous plant oils. The end of July was lost to me in this way, and it seems this will be the dowry of the new month as well.

I keep inside as much as my soul can stand seclusion, and live outside as much as my body can take it. Blazing, cloudless waves of heat aggravate the itching provoked by poison ivy, which, I should say, has become a nuisance to me, as much as my body is resisting its effects.

But how can one refrain from coming here with so many cardinals navigating the air? And how can one resist not visiting the overgrown border of privets—more lush and verdant than ever, and bursting with branches sweeping down to the grass with white veils of fragrant flowers?

Somewhere beyond the stream, from the heart of that jumble of branches and trees and shrubbery, comes the almost petrifying and awesome sound of hundreds of winged armies—the cicadas singing their summer songs. I am mystified by the persistence of these creatures, which never cease their soundtrack, as if seeking to know if God understands their idioms.

My father and I have planted hundreds of gladiolus bulbs together in this garden. He'd prepare a space for each bulb with his hoe, and I would bury each bulb in the womb of the earth. I will always be reminded of him with the fondest of memories whenever the shades of late summer stalks burst from the ground in colorful intonation—a song of remembrance, hope, labor, and deep-rooted love.

Talking to the Father

Dear heavenly Father, I confer all my deepest gratitude to You for the exultant hours of summer and songs nurtured in my heart of hearts. I am no more than a speck of dust in the expanse of time. But I am more than that. I am the end result of a dream, the name embroidered in Your heart since the beginning of time, waiting to be just what You intend me to be.

> Dear friends,
> now we are children
> of God, and what we
> will be has not yet been
> made known.
> But we know that when
> Christ appears,
> we shall be like him,
> for we shall see him
> as he is.
> —1 John 3:2, NIV

August

Sleeping in the Garden

We are sleeping in the garden again. Under the grapevine-covered porch, we have improvised a bed using reclaimed hardwood for a frame and a spare mattress.

Darkness descends slowly upon us every evening. With the last light of day, the enthralling songs of night creatures grow louder. Shadows take tangible forms, and down the garden path, choruses of crickets initiate the extravaganza of the night, filling us with wonder and silent prayers each time. From our transitory bed, I can see the moon gliding through the night amid tree branches, always regal in her distant beauty, like a queen among her shiny maidens, the stars.

Last night, right after the evening progressed into the deep shadows of night, the unexpected music of a lonesome cricket, hiding somewhere amid the hand-sized leaves of the grapevine, floated to my ears. I listened to his nocturnal melodies until, finally, my thoughts grew silent and sweet sleep washed my spirit clean in the forgetfulness of unconsciousness.

In many ways, our precious world still mirrors Adam and Eve's glorious Garden of Eden at the beginning of Creation. I can only imagine the magnificence and splendor of our future dwellings in heaven: homes where walls and roofs will allow the display of God's glory reflected in the beauty of the renewed earth.

The fulfillment of God's plan for His earthly children has taken longer than we may have expected or liked, but we should keep the flame of hope alive. We're not to be thwarted by disappointment, because faithful is He who has promised.

God's Words
"He always stands by his covenant—the commitment he made to a thousand generations" (Psalm 105:8, NLT).

To Everything There Is a Season

The new morning begins like a dream filled with the promise of wonderful things. On my kitchen table, the plum-colored flowers of the smoke bush placed in a vintage hand-painted pitcher bestow the room with an old-world feel, but outside everything is again under the heat, waiting for a second chance.

This is the time for some of the perennials in the garden to shine. Although by now many flowers have finished blooming, and others are beginning to look a little ragged around the edges under the heat of August, others are just beginning to bloom.

Each early August morning is filled with the delightful fragrances wafting from the bigheaded, tall phlox plants in lovely white, pink, and violet flowerets. The long-stemmed cutting flowers, such as the zinnias, are hitting their peak bloom. Garden mums, the China aster, and the deliciously scented sweet autumn clematis, by now covered in lovely, tiny white blossoms, will brighten the late summer garden until they are killed by frost.

> To everything
> there is a season,
> A time for every purpose
> under heaven.
> —Ecclesiastes 3:1, NKJV

> But my garden teaches me that as sure
> as the natural world keeps its timing, we can be certain that
> the promise of Jesus' return is more than a mere wish,
> a fanciful dream, or a figment of our imagination.

My garden is a constant reminder that to everything there is a season, and a time to every purpose under heaven. Timing was also important in Jesus' life. At the very least, He seemed very conscious of timing. In more than one instance, He punctuated His statements with "My time has not yet come."

We tend to get easily discouraged when things don't go as we'd planned, or when our efforts are not making a difference. Many true Christians in today's world are discouraged by God's apparent delay. We desperately long for Christ's return—not only as the fulfillment of His promises but also as the deliverance from pain and our ultimate enemy: death.

But my garden teaches me that as sure as the natural world keeps its timing, we can be certain that the promise of Jesus' return is more than a mere wish, a fanciful dream, or a figment of our imagination. It is a firm reality, under God's own timing.

> There will be no more death or tears.

Reflect:

ᴥ What signs of Jesus' soon return do I observe around me today?

_____

_____

ᴥ How can I share the good news of Jesus' return with someone today?

_____

_____

God's Words

"Then will appear the sign of the Son of Man in heaven. And then all the peoples of the earth will mourn when they see the Son of Man coming on the clouds of heaven, with power and great glory. And he will send his angels with a loud trumpet call, and they will gather his elect from the four winds, from one end of the heavens to the other" (Matthew 24:30, 31, NIV).

God's Presence in the Garden

There's a sense of newness all round me. A freshness under imperturbable blue summer skies. This rebirth of the natural world, and the miraculous resurrection that has each shrub, tree, and flower singing its own praises, has renewed my hunger for new beginnings, a new world undaunted by sin.

All this is a result of an unexpected change in climate and the cool temperatures that have graced us for the past few days, bringing needed healing and endless mercies to the garden. Thus, I'd found myself watering and weeding my little world clad in my favorite old pink sweater again. What marvelous, marvelous weather—and such a fine change from the loathsome heat of the past few weeks.

> But will God indeed dwell on the earth? Behold, heaven and the heaven of heavens cannot contain You. How much less this temple which I have built!
> —1 Kings 8:27, NKJV

Rosebushes have sprung back to life and are heavy with buds, ready to bloom in another succession of spectacular mauves and amethysts and icy whites. Birds appear happier too. They seem to fly with a renewed zest.

A feathered friend (I wonder which one, among so many) left me a very special gift hidden among leaves of emerald this morning: a luminous, multi-color feather in bright greens and toasted yellows. The garden feels wonderfully quiet, and so wonderfully beautiful as the western tanager up on the highest branch of the flowering pear tree starts warbling a most enchanting piece. The Anna's hummingbird that's been visiting my garden this summer is once again fluttering about the honeysuckle vine with wings so swift, it almost looks unreal.

> There's not a better place to experience
> God's presence than in the garden.

Last evening, I filled all the bird feeders, and birds have already been discovering them. Above my head, the airways are already busy. Happy twirling and chirpings and guttural songs fill the morning air with blessings and thanksgiving. What a treasure birds are! They're such amazing creatures.

There's not a better place to experience God's presence than in the garden. But there are special times when I feel His closeness in even greater measure. On those occasions, I will stop whatever it is I may be doing and look up, my whole being listening to the song of trees as their burly, scraggy arms reach the heavens, and their shaggy green heads bend together in humble prayer. *Are You here, God? Are You here?*

In wonder and admiration, I keep listening for the voice of God in the music made by tree branches and breezes. Humility and awe fill my very being until I like the trees of the field, stretch out my arms to the Creator of all and recommit myself to Him again and again and again.

God's Words
"Come near to God and he will come near to you" (James 4:8, NIV).

Reflect
∾ How is God revealing Himself to you as you spend time in His creation?

_____

_____

_____

Listen for the voice of God.

My Presence Will Go With You

Our garden is still bursting with life and color. Flawless skies are the heavenly cloak gently extended over the world. From where I am sitting, at the large square table writing about these joys, my little world looks like an aviary. Windows are wide open, and as ruffles of curtains dance solemnly in the morning breeze, I can hear the birds serenading the day with their signature songs.

Birds are making waves as they fly from tree to tree like the professional surfers of the air they are. From my peripheral vision, I catch sight of a vivid splash of yellow against the greenery and marvel at the capriciousness of nature. It seems like only yesterday the western tanagers were just drab little birds among the many swallows feeding from the bird feeders outside the kitchen window. But the dullness of their winter coat has been shed, and lately their bright yellow plumage has been a shot of joy to the soul, and their tinkling canary-like song has been like feathers caressing my ear.

> And He is busy feeding the birds of the field
> just as his Holy Spirit enriches and fills my life
> with hope and assurance.

These little birds are indeed some of the best surfers of the air. The pull of gravity is not a concern. They make invisible ripples as they plunge into the air and ride the winds, creating the illusion of a scoop in a wave, or the perfect barrel that surfers ride. Their flight is so swift, and they are so attuned to the air under their wings, that I cannot help but smile in amazement of these little creatures.

A shaft of the purest ray of sunlight hits my picnic table, and I catch

> And he said,
> My presence
> shall go with thee,
> and I will give thee rest.
> —Exodus 33:14, KJV

sudden wafts of the sweet scent of honeysuckle. I'm certain that God walks in my garden. He has been silently unfolding new buds these days. And He is busy feeding the birds of the field just as his Holy Spirit enriches and fills my life with hope and assurance.

God's Words

> Where can I go from your Spirit?
> > Where can I flee from your presence?
> If I go up to the heavens, you are there;
> > if I make my bed in the depths, you are there.
> If I rise on the wings of the dawn,
> > if I settle on the far side of the sea,
> even there your hand will guide me,
> > your right hand will hold me fast
> (Psalm 139:7–10, NIV).

Reflect

ɷ How does your perspective on today change as you recognize God's presence?

_____

_____

_____

_____

ɷ What promises are building your hope and faith today?

_____

_____

_____

_____

The Eternal God, Our Refuge

Birds have taken over our porch. It has to do with the lush grapevine that has practically covered our porch in curtains of ripe green grapes. It's like living inside nature. Where would you live if you were a bird?

If you could fly and make your house in furtive high places, what tree would you choose among the many? Would you choose a knothole in a branch for your home? Would you choose a large crack in a dry trunk, or would you nest in a rotting pile of vegetation? Would you prefer a mud dome with a long entryway, a cozy tunnel in the ground, or a wide sill on a building? What would you choose, if you were a bird?

> The eternal God is your refuge, and underneath are the everlasting arms.
> —Deuteronomy 33:27, NIV

My heart is a like a chickadee searching for its home.

There is a luxuriant island of trees in my neighbor's backyard diagonally across from our garden that captivates me. It's a cluster of gnarled and twisted trees with interestingly curled branches that almost top the highest roofs of the neighborhood. I can see these trees from all corners of our backyard. They remind me of fairy tales and children's stories from my childhood—knotted and twisted as they are, and as mysterious as they can be in an urban garden.

There's a gentle kind of hush to these trees that enchant me. In the smoothness and delicacy of thin, curly branches, in the outer reaches of thin leaves and wide canopies, in the way they sway under tender breezes—they have the power to ignite my imagination.

Birds and other wildlife seem to love this intricate clump of trees as much as I do, for more than one species find their habitat there. If I were a bird, I would choose the gnarled trees in my neighbor's backyard as my dwelling place. My heart is a like a chickadee searching for its home.

Talking to the Father

Father, only in You do I find my place of safety. You are my refuge, protection, food, and the place where I want to live and raise my family. Let us not forget our resting place (see Jeremiah 50:6).

God is my refuge and resting place.

Reflect

꙾ How is God revealing Himself as my place of safety today?

_____

_____

_____

꙾ What am I thankful for today?

_____

_____

_____

꙾ What comfort does knowing that God is your Home bring you today?

_____

_____

_____

_____

_____

_____

Kneeling Before the Father

Like some fascinated yellow butterfly, joyfulness swirls all around and about me. It is almost a tangible thing. A jewel within me, this joy is. It has to do with a gratitude-filled heart and also, I'm sure, with this new coolness in which the early morning seems to be awakening to of lately, allowing us a blessed respite from the intense heat that has besieged us for several consecutive weeks.

The weather has mellowed in a sudden taste of fall, with chilly mornings melted in golden globules of sunshine. I sit quietly out here, allowing my mind to be filled with the awareness of God's presence and letting my heart treasure all I see and hear.

How very lovely and wonderful it feels out here in the garden! There is beauty everywhere I look. Even leaves carry in their hues the almost unnoticeable but true signs of the near future, impending as autumn is.

All around me, I see that sunshine is dappling trees and the garden floor with polka dots. Within my heart there shimmers a little light too. Above me—where shaggy green tree canopies sway in gentle breezes—I find what the naked eye alone cannot see. Only the trusting heart knows it all too well: God's Spirit hovers over me. He hems me in behind and before. His hand is upon me. God is near. I've stumbled again into the Great I AM. I am overcome by this knowledge. This consciousness of God's presence places in my heart a yearning for the day when we will embrace God's fullness.

> You hem me in behind and before,
> and you lay your hand upon me.
> Such knowledge is too wonderful for me,
> too lofty for me to attain.
> —Psalm 139:5, 6, NIV

God's Words

"For this reason I kneel before the Father, from whom every family in heaven and on earth derives its name. I pray that out of his glorious riches he may strengthen you with power through his Spirit in your inner being, so that Christ may dwell in your hearts through faith. And I pray that you, being rooted and established in love, may have power, together with all the Lord's holy people, to grasp how wide and long and high and deep is the love of Christ, and to know this love that surpasses knowledge—that you may be filled to the measure of all the fullness of God" (Ephesians 3:14–19, NIV).

August

Teach Us to Number Our Days

I cut some hydrangea flowerets this morning and arranged them into lovely bouquets that I placed around the house, filling it with the colors and imageries of sultry, summery days.

Over at the entrance of the garden, the tall Shasta daisies, in their unruly little patch, have decided that they shall be happier on the floor, and thus, their tall, slim bodies have bent down and taken half the pathway in graceful waves of white. I love the freshness and purity of the Shasta daisies. Even after they've been trimmed off and put in the trash, these happy little flowers still retain their power to make us smile.

> I cut some hydrangea flowerets this morning
> and arranged them into lovely bouquets
> that I placed around the house.

There are grapevines growing in several places of the garden, along with Virginia creeper and others. Vines are such mysterious things to me. Perhaps it's the lush green of their foliage that enthralls me, or maybe it's the association they have in books and old stories with shady and secluded places, abandoned castles, and dappled places deep in the forest. Perhaps it's just the way they have of reaching out to things, impossibly clinging everywhere: their leaves, fruit clusters, flowers, shoots, canes, and tendrils coiling around fences and other objects with arms and hands and fingers. Living things they are, indeed.

Around this time of the year, the grapevines have grown into quite an impressive sight. They're living screens, walls, and roofs. They have barricaded the back porch, making it feel dark and cozy and a perfect place to sit, relax, and dream summer dreams.

> Teach us
> to number our days,
> that we may gain
> a heart of wisdom.
> —Psalm 90:12, NIV

I am almost certain that the grapevine growing on our back porch knows me and even rejoices when it sees me. If not, why would it stir and move and stretch out thin arms and long fingers to grab my hair whenever I pass by it? I can almost hear it laughing at me as strands of my hair get caught on grabby green fingers.

Later, at the end of the day, I will again stumble upon my prayer place by our bedroom window, for a moment surveying the horizon in search of the departing sun. I did not see it today, though, sheltered as it was by the tall trees sheltering our east-facing window; but I knew it was still up there somewhere. The sun is a lovely ruler of the natural world, and from my window prayer chapel, I delight in recording its journey throughout the day. Its faithfulness never ceases to amaze me.

Every day is a gift to enjoy.

Reflect

❧ In what ways do you recognize God teaching you wisdom today?

_____

_____

_____

_____

_____

_____

God's Words

"From the rising of the sun to the place where it sets, the name of the LORD is to be praised" (Psalm 113:3, NIV).

WELCOME

September

By all these lovely tokens
September days are here,
With summer's best of weather,
And autumn's best of cheer.
—Helen Hunt Jackson

Heavenly Evidences

The minute I stepped into the garden this morning, I felt it—the crisp nippiness exuding from frosty blue skies, the tingling in my veins brought on by the prospect of autumnal delights brewing on the horizon. The wheel of time keeps on turning. We're standing on the threshold of a dying season, and nature is reminding us again that the sweet smell of summer is fleeting.

Seasons come and seasons go almost imperceptibly, but some things cannot go ignored. Nature speaks. It leaves a trail of signs, natural warnings, and methods too obvious to disregard. As it is, I am already collecting shreds of memories made on a season that is now departing. Against the horizon, behind the mountain to the far northwest, winter is slowly creeping up on us.

The clues that give away nature's plans have inspired many throughout the ages. Still today, clues and signs found in nature are useful in many ways. From helping us define the meaning of atmospheric changes and how they affect us to understanding what frightening creatures may be lurking around our property and our children or what's devouring our harvest under the cover of darkness, signs and clues in nature have much to teach us, if we only pay attention to our surroundings.

> In the presence of God and of Christ Jesus, who will judge the living and the dead, and in view of his appearing and his kingdom, I give you this charge: Preach the word; be prepared in season and out of season.
> —2 Timothy 4:1, 2, NIV

In the same way He does with nature, God gives us clues and signs to guide us through life's journey.

In the same way He does with nature, God gives us clues and signs to guide us through life's journey. Some of God's most important clues and warning signs have to do with His return to earth and the timing of the end. Our human race is now uniquely poised on the precipice of time, where no generation has ever stood. We are living in the days spoken of by the ancient prophets. Yet a whole array of distractions is blinding us from deciphering the signs so loudly proclaimed in the pages of our time.

We see the clues. We see the signs. We hear God whispering on the winds of history. Yet unbelievers persist in saying, "Where is the promise of His coming? For since the fathers fell asleep, all things continue as they were from the beginning of creation" (2 Peter 3:4, NKJV).

Talking to the Father

Dear Father, just like You have supplied the signs found in the natural world, You have given us many signs suggest that Your return is very near. Help us live so close to You that our hearts won't become oblivious to what is irrefutably obvious.

Reflect

ᴥ How does the reality of Jesus' soon return affect the way I live my life today?

_____

_____

_____

_____

ᴥ What evidence of Christ's soon return do I see today?

_____

_____

_____

_____

God's Words

"As it was in the days of Noah, so it will be at the coming of the Son of Man. For in the days before the flood, people were eating and drinking, marrying and giving in marriage, up to the day Noah entered the ark; and they knew nothing about what would happen until the flood came and took them all away. That is how it will be at the coming of the Son of Man" (Matthew 24:37–39, NIV).

What is God telling you to do while you await His return?

God's Loving Hand Upon the Earth

There is still such an abundance of color in the garden that it's hard to believe summer is fading into fall. The rosebushes are bursting with buds that promise many fragrant bouquets for days to come. Only the carpet of the few crisp brown leaves under my feet as I go about the garden give any indication that autumn is practically here. It's a lovely overlapping of seasons.

The Sally Holmes climbing rose is still intent on covering the garden's northeastern wall in one last rush of glory—long, slender shoots with massive clusters of white and pale pinks draping over our bedroom window. Its rosettes resemble hydrangea heads.

Under the same beds where these roses grow also dwell miraculous little plants: the snapdragons, ruffled and showy in bright shades of carmine, crimson, yellow, maroon, orange, and red—supposedly annuals, yet insisting on coming back a little stronger each year—lovely and perfect in their own right. Dozens of wispy yellow butterflies hover over these dramatic two-lipped flowers, as well as the phlox and black-eyed Susans standing on the west side. So deeply involved in sipping nectar are the butterflies that one can almost seize them with ease.

The garden resembles a sweet jumble of muted greens, yellows, reds, and mauves, and the tall grasses seem to have forgotten that the natural world is about to go dormant. I marvel and rejoice in everything that surrounds me. In all that I see and feel, I sense God's loving hand. My heart has been captivated by God's creation. I welcome the mellow months of the year with open arms and a heart overflowing with love for the Almighty, in total anticipation of what He's yet to do in me.

> And why do you worry about clothes? See how the flowers of the field grow. They do not labor or spin. Yet I tell you that not even Solomon in all his splendor was dressed like one of these.
> —Matthew 6:28, 29, NIV

God's Words

"Take delight in the LORD, and he will give you the desires of your heart" (Psalm 37:4, NIV).

September

The Crimson Hues of September

If you'd look up to where the autumn-crimsoned heads of maples and aspens sway, softly stirred by gentle breezes, you would notice it. There, through the spaces in their canopies, the sun shines directly over certain parts of the garden in a downpour of light—soft, autumnal light.

The scorching heat of summer has fled, and temperatures, subdued now by balmier weather, have mellowed the garden. I welcome these marvelous, temperate September days. The air is sweet, and the woods beyond the garden hum a new kind of song.

I hear, too, coming from the bramble beyond the garden, a rustle, a cackle—the scraping sound of the curve-billed thrasher, flogging the soil with its big sickle-shaped bill, rooting out insects. I then stop in my tracks and listen, wondering if perhaps the elusive covey of bluish-gray California quail I saw just the other day around the garden is foraging for food in that same patch of woods.

You would expect to feel some annoyance as leaves fall from trees and summer fades behind the crimson hues of September, but how can I, when everything in the garden is bursting with such beauty! I shall embrace each moment, this last hurrah of summer. Thus, these days I've been a spirit drifting through the tall reaches of aspens and birches lining the edge of the garden. A woman praying on wings of birds, or sitting on a bed of grass, or dreaming by the shimmer of the autumn's twilight. A woman in pursuit of God's presence through what she sees and finds around her in the work of His hands.

And where her heart wanders, there, too, follows God. For she knows that her Redeemer is close behind—even when she questions the heavens and her spirit wrestles with doubts.

Talking to the Father

Dear heavenly Father, few things can be more disheartening and destructive to faith than the feeling that You don't hear our prayers or care for us. It is easy to come to such conclusions when we feel we're not getting a response from You. But we have known You from the depths of our fears; through our infirmities we have learned that You are a God who listens and empathizes with our weaknesses. Your love overflows in goodness. You are our sustenance, and we thank You beforehand for the many blessings You are about to bestow upon us.

Reflect

∾ How am I pursuing God today?

_____

_____

_____

_____

Invite God
to walk beside you
every day.

∾ What am I thankful for today?

_____

_____

_____

_____

God's Words

"Am I only a God nearby,"
　　declares the LORD,
"and not a God far away?
Who can hide in secret places
　　so that I cannot see them?"
　　declares the LORD.
"Do not I fill heaven and earth?"
　　declares the LORD
(Jeremiah 23:23, 24, NIV).

September

Light in the Darkness

We woke up this morning to the sound of rain. From the partially open window on my right, an ashen slice of sky filtered through, inviting me to linger a little longer. I rejoiced in the comforting heaviness hanging from musky skies outside, and, clinging to the warmth and comfort of my bed, decided to sleep a little longer. But the loud clatter of raindrops on gutters and rooftops had other plans for my morning. The gentle noise swept away whatever traces of lethargy remained and had me going even before the day had time to fully awake.

A whiff of marigolds infused with the scent of rain and dampened earth wafts in from the garden, now silent and looking forlorn under the veil of rain. I supposed it must have been waiting for the miracle of light to soothe its wretched heart. Thus, as if I could help lift any despondency, I hurried about the house, turning on lights here and there.

Light, like glimmering stars of hope and benevolence, pushes back against the gloominess of cloudy mornings.

Soon, the hurricane lantern, table lamps, and candles were illuminating the rainy, autumnal day. Soft light twinkled on objects, drawing fantastical shapes and funny figures on walls, floors, and ceilings. Light always knows how to lift my spirit as it scatters away untamed shadows. Light, like glimmering stars of hope and benevolence, pushes back against the gloominess of cloudy mornings.

How precious is light! And how spontaneously and genuinely it comes into our lives, isolating shadows and illuminating sad, darkened corners.

Talking to the Father
O Lord, my life is like a speck of dust. My voice like a crashing raindrop that resonates through the silent night, echoing my neediness. May You be the Light that shines in my darkness, bringing hope and precious assurance to my life.

As Clearly as God Sees Us

It always happens after a rainy night. It is called fog. You look outside your window, and you're immediately enveloped in it—dense, muffled sheets of white stretching throughout the drowsy landscape as far as your eyes can see.

You may think that this phenomenon has a life in itself, as it seems to rise from the depths of the earth like some divine and mysterious incense draping the morning with cool, wet embraces. Fog widens over the roughness of the land and then, again, up the hill that creates a parapet next to our little white cottage, creating a fortress in the midst of this ashen vastness, and again up the tips of oaks and maples that, on mornings like this, are but silent sentinels and faithful pillars of the earth.

> I can always find my Creator cocooning my soul
> and my moments with tenderness and care.

There's an ethereal beauty in fog that I don't see in other weather conditions. I am in awe of nature's capriciousness. Beauty beckons to be found, even under the least favorable circumstances. How wonderfully beautiful this earth is. How precious are these hazy mornings, this sacred revelry of my damp little world, where above all my cares I can always find my Creator cocooning my soul and my moments with tenderness and care.

Reflect

ᴏ How is God revealing His tenderness to you today?

_____

_____

_____

> We don't yet see
> things clearly.
> We're squinting
> in a fog,
> peering through a mist.
> But it won't be long
> before the weather
> clears and the
> sun shines bright!
> We'll see it all then,
> see it all as clearly
> as God sees us,
> knowing him directly just
> as he knows us!
> —1 Corinthians 13:12, *The Message*

September

Do Not Lose Heart

The garden is quickly weakening under the crispy hand of late September. Leaves and vegetation are changing from bright emerald greens to the washed-out, parchment-like colors of fall. Although there's still much beauty to be found in the garden, it is an opaque and vulnerable kind of glory. It is a beauty that can only predict its own end, for it is to linger here only for a while.

The garden is a tired old man, and I can hear the lonely cry of his heart: "Even when I am old and gray, do not forsake me, my God, till I declare your power to the next generation, your mighty acts to all who are to come" (Psalm 71:18, NIV).

As the late summer garden shrouds itself in this unconscious prelude to death, I think of my own mortality. I am also a frightened leaf trembling in the wind. I need to take heed of the natural world and listen to what it has to teach me.

> God wants to bless our finite earthly existence with honor, wisdom, strength, and spiritual abundance.

Beyond the natural processes of aging and decay, God promises uncountable blessings to those who trust Him. We will be sustained in the fall season of our lives. God wants to bless our finite earthly existence with honor, wisdom, strength, and spiritual abundance. But what's even more important is the clear understanding and assurance of His continual presence in our lives.

God the Son is well acquainted with our qualms. He understands our fears and fragilities. Through His servant, the prophet Isaiah, He assures us of His concern for us: "Even to your old age and gray hairs I am he, I am he who will sustain you. I have made you and I will carry you; I will sustain you and I will rescue you" (Isaiah 46:4, NIV).

God Shall Wipe Away All Tears

There's a feeling of deliciousness under clear blue skies and mornings clad in the color of russet sunshine. Deliciousness under giant trees way above a little white cottage and the girl with wild hair who lives under their canopies. And a delicious, obliging warmth with a golden-brown tad of nippiness in it. How marvelous these glorious autumn days are to me! And how glorious the feelings and thoughts they bring into my heart!

I think of family and friends reunited, of wind songs on quivering leaves, and of russet showers of dried leaves rushing down from somnolent branches. And in the house, the scents and tastes of pumpkin spice, freshly picked apples, cinnamon, and cloves, and the glow of lamps through windows and candles flickering—all are sure signs that autumn is fluttering about my little world, like some welcoming butterfly.

It's the time of the shift, the symbolic embrace of summer and autumn, the sky in transition, summer transitioning into fall. All speak to my heart in profound ways. Fall certainly is a favorite season to many. But the dying season won't forget she has a message to convey and insists in reminding us of our own mortality with punitive candor.

How comforting to the anxious heart the promises of Christ are: "Listen, I tell you a mystery: We will not all sleep, but we will all be changed—in a flash, in the twinkling of an eye, at the last trumpet. For the trumpet will sound, the dead will be raised imperishable, and we will be changed" (1 Corinthians 15:51, 52, NIV).

Talking to the Father
Come, Lord Jesus!

And God shall wipe away all tears from their eyes; and there shall be no more death, neither sorrow, nor crying, neither shall there be any more pain: for the former things are passed away.
—Revelation 21:4, KJV

September

How Majestic Is Your Name

I work in the garden, and my heart wonders. I sweep dead leaves and fluff up cushions on the outdoor furniture while my mouth sings a joyful song. And I wonder and marvel and sing to the massive trees circling our little cottage as a fortress and to the dozen butterflies with wings like orange China paper hovering over the zinnia beds.

I water roses and talk to the birds. I pull out capricious weeds. I fill bird feeders and clean their floors of food debris left by greedy squirrels. And I marvel and praise and thank the Great I AM, who speaks to my heart through such an array of wonders.

My days are melting away in dreams of pink and purple petals. My soul dances the hours away on tippy toes. I'm growing wings under my breath, and pansies in the hollow of my hands.

> In no better place do I find the fingerprints of God
> as clearly as in the natural world.

God speaks to me through creation and plants poetry under my tongue. He speaks when I look up at the stars on crispy nights and stroll through my wildflower garden under the September sun. In no better place do I find the fingerprints of God as clearly as in the natural world.

The more I take pleasure in the wonder of creation, the more I am convinced of God's sovereignty. God doesn't just speak through the order and design we find in creation but also through the outstanding beauty that surrounds us. Nature doesn't just corroborate God's existence, it also proves that our Creator is indeed an artist without peer. It is no wonder the beloved nature-lover king of Israel, David, was able to write such inspiring compositions:

The heavens declare the glory of God;
 the skies proclaim the work of his hands.
Day after day they pour forth speech;
 night after night they reveal knowledge.
They have no speech, they use no words;
 no sound is heard from them.
Yet their voice goes out into all the earth,
 their words to the ends of the world.
In the heavens God has pitched a tent for the sun.
 It is like a bridegroom coming out of his chamber,
 like a champion rejoicing to run his course.
It rises at one end of the heavens
 and makes its circuit to the other;
 nothing is deprived of its warmth (Psalm 19:1–6, NIV).

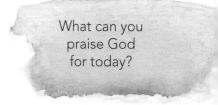

What can you praise God for today?

Reflect

∾ How is God speaking to me today?

_____

_____

_____

∾ Where do I see the fingerprints of God today?

_____

_____

_____

_____

September

Autumnal Days

The flying jewels of the garden, the ruby-throated hummingbirds, have vanished overnight. They left the garden a week or two ago. I wonder what paths these amazing creatures take on their long winter journeys and if the airways in their avian world are as busy and overcrowded this time of year as our train stations and airports and buses are in our own human world during the holidays.

The garden has dressed down a bit these days, but although its flowery beauty and radiant splendor is not as exuberant as it was just a few weeks ago, there reigns in it a peaceful glory hardly exceeded by any other season. The migrating birds, finding tasty treats in the bird feeders, have invaded the back porch. Their antics at the feeders under the arch covered by the moonflower vine make a precious sight for the eyes and the soul.

I am amazed by the impressive variety of birds uniting in one spot at any time of day. Today, I observe a meeting of brown thrashers, blue jays, cardinals, mockingbirds, and tufted titmice.

Small wild rabbits, too, allowing their great sense of smell to guide them, have herded over to our gardens, where the wild onions have returned and are now blooming like grass. I love watching these cute creatures munching their day away or hopping around the garden in their fairy-tale gait. There's no doubt in my mind that once upon a time, rabbits visited Lewis Carroll in his garden. Surely, these lovely autumn days ignite imagination and imbue the spirit with thoughts of wonder and delight.

Our souls, too, wait upon the Lord.
Our hearts are alight with the hope of Christ's return to earth.

The autumnal winds have also brought in the late butterflies. Are they on their way to some warmer little plot of land somewhere south? There's a riot of them these days over where the tall zinnias are past their glory and where the tiny tubelike trumpet flowers of the cypress vine intertwine and creep up, quietly fading away.

I wait in expectation for the return of the mourning dove to the garden, for I haven't seen them throughout the long, hot summer days; they should be coming to the winter feeders any day now, seeking refuge. Our souls, too, wait upon the Lord. Our hearts are alight with the hope of Christ's return to earth. This is indeed the season to rekindle the hope in God's promises and the season to remember that the entire universe is interested in seeing us grow in faith and perseverance as we learn to wait upon the Lord.

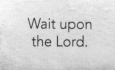

Wait upon the Lord.

Talking to the Father

I thank You, Lord, for the beauty with which You have surrounded us on this earth, so that we may know You and come to love You.

Reflect

∾ How does God's unchanging nature bring you hope today?

_____

_____

_____

_____

_____

God's Words

"And let the peace of Christ rule in your hearts, to which indeed you were called in one body. And be thankful. Let the word of Christ dwell in you richly, teaching and admonishing one another in all wisdom, singing psalms and hymns and spiritual songs, with thankfulness in your hearts to God" (Colossians 3:15, 16, ESV).

September

And They Will Rise Again

I clipped the last of the roses this morning. How lovely and perfect those late blooms are upon the autumnal landscape. I have always loved this period of unseasonably warm, dry weather before autumn's frosty fingers finally put the garden to sleep.

I'm going to miss my roses. I will miss seeing them embellishing the house in tarnished silver vases and humble jars. But the death of the garden is just a peaceful, unconscious waiting for spring. I will see my roses again.

These late-in-the-season roses are reminiscent of dear old friends to me. Friends and family from whom it's always hard to part. We miss them when they leave. We miss their laughter, miss their presence, and always long for a prompt reunion.

> Just like the sleeping roses in the garden always wake up again when touched by the warmth of sunny spring days, the dead shall rise again at God's command, restored in beauty and joy.

There's so much comfort in God's words when it comes to death. It is always hard to deal with separation, but we can rest assured that even death is not the final goodbye. Just like the sleeping roses in the garden always wake up again when touched by the warmth of sunny spring days, the dead shall rise again at God's command, restored in beauty and joy. Death is just a peaceful, unconscious sleep, waiting for resurrection.

We can cherish the hope that we will be reunited with our loved ones one day. "Weeping may endure for a night, but joy cometh in the morning" (Psalm 30:5, KJV).

"A Farewell"

Summer wanes . . .
Summer dwindles away . . .
Summer sings a final hymn and paints the sky with brilliant flair . . .
Summer is a hopping rabbit getting ready for winter,
And a wee baby turtle dreaming on the last magical grass-green leaf.
Day wanes into shadowy fields,
Enchanted gardens fill with singing . . .
I am ready.
My heart embraces the hope of autumn.
I walk in the garden and wait for the falling leaf.
October's early embrace swirls around me . . .
Like a grasshopper's horn I hear it;
High in the maples, its voice rings.
I am a dancing leaf,
A new month murmurs its mute benediction over my soul,
While I gaze at a garden so ready to sleep.
Welcome October!
—Olga Valdivia

WELCOME

October

I'm so glad I live in a world
where there are Octobers.
–L. M. Montgomery

They Who Wait for the Lord

The garden has started to settle down into its rest. Its scent is sweet and reminiscent of all the goodness of the autumnal season: the first fire in the fireplace, beeswax candles on the dinner table as night's darkness falls earlier and earlier, and the scent of apple trees, pickling spices, cinnamon, and nutmeg.

Trees and flowerless bushes rest quietly under the gentle peace of crimsoned days, and toast-colored leaves swirl and dance with the winds that blow through sleepy branches, bringing in whispers from beyond the unknown.

The sky is sweet and bright, like cotton candy; each cloud festooned in puffy tutus of shell pinks and muted blues, and nights confess their own glories. Our little white cottage is a tiny bright light under the new darkness of the season.

I am captivated by the peaceful beauty of autumn. October produces so pleasant an effect on my feelings. Under its golden light, I am a little girl, dancing in the garden with a sanctified heart, filled with gratitude and thanksgiving.

This is the season of hair blowing wild in cool breezes, crunchy leaf showers, and neighboring feral cats wandering the silent gardens. This is the season of quiet dinners by the fire, fluffy feather beds on cold nights, and a house smelling of cinnamon, oranges, and cloves. It is the time to enjoy simplicity and remain conscious of God's nearness.

George Eliot wrote,

> But they who wait
> for the LORD shall
> renew their strength;
> they shall mount up
> with wings like eagles;
> they shall run
> and not be weary;
> they shall walk
> and not faint.
> —Isaiah 40:31, ESV

"Delicious autumn!
My very soul is wedded to it, and if I were a bird
I would fly about the earth
seeking the successive autumns."

God's Words

"For everything there is a season, and a time for every matter under heaven:

a time to be born, and a time to die;
a time to plant, and a time to pluck up what is planted;
a time to kill, and a time to heal;
a time to break down, and a time to build up;
a time to weep, and a time to laugh;
a time to mourn, and a time to dance;
a time to cast away stones, and a time to gather stones together;
a time to embrace, and a time to refrain from embracing"

(Ecclesiastes 3:1–5, ESV).

The Night Garden

The night garden: A yellow moon hangs forlornly over the deep indigo sky. Dark shadows creep quietly on vines and tree branches that have started to lose the last of their leaves. As I walk slowly, shrouded in moonlight, the night air brings to my attentive ears the muted sounds and whispers of the dark and the haunting sensation of not belonging.

The nocturnal garden has a changed anatomy. This dear, all-too-familiar place of my summer days—now dark and cheerless by night—has become strange. Every step I take in its shadows speaks of change and decay.

It is hard to remember that only this morning the garden had been a sanctuary, alive with birds and freshly fallen leaves forming heaps of gold scattered under trees. The grass is still springy, inviting me to walk on it and maybe even sleep on its downy surface. But the shadows of night, tiptoeing over the horizon, have come earlier. Down from tree branches, they descended and crept throughout the garden's floor, making all sorts of changes to my daytime dreamscape.

He never changes
or casts
a shifting shadow.
—James 1:17, NLT

> Changes. I dislike changes. Even changes meant
> for the better sometimes bring drawbacks and uneasiness.

Changes. I dislike changes. Even changes meant for the better sometimes bring drawbacks and uneasiness. Today is my birthday, and I can also foresee changes in the landscape of my life.

Middle adulthood is also a season of change. It is a time of contemplation and evaluation. We still look to the days ahead, but we are becoming increasingly frightened by the realization that we will not be around forever.

But amid the frustrations and fears brought by impending change, it is comforting to know that God never changes. The circumstances that cause change in us have no effect on God.

God is the same
yesterday, today,
and tomorrow.

Reflect

∾ How does God's unchangeableness affect my hope and faith?

_____

_____

∾ Today I am thankful for:

_____

_____

God's Words

"Jesus Christ is the same yesterday and today and forever" (Hebrews 13:8, ESV).

Golden Sunshine

My heart is overflowing with thankfulness and humble gratitude. I am thankful for days aglow with golden sunshine, crimsoned leaves scattered on wet grasses, the sound of crows swooping and calling, and the grapevine clinging to the fence with naked fingers. Grateful, too, for these past joyful days of reunion and family happiness.

The security and constancy of love from precious family members are such rich blessings to me. There's nothing I value more than the closeness of family and the circle of strength and love they represent. But these few days of happy companionship are finally coming to an end. And as I say my good-byes, my heart becomes guilty of the same gloominess and despondency of the October garden.

I always feel this frightful sensation of emptiness when I have to part from those I love. There is a sadness in every goodbye, something akin to the slow death of the October garden and the increased isolation brought by the passing of summer.

Absence from those whom we love is a small death. We carry within our soul this primordial fear of separation. We yearn for a future that will forever preserve our connection with our loved ones. Because of sin, we live with the fear of absolute separation, a dread so profound that we must keep it deeply shut within ourselves, so as not to have our souls faint.

Nature's classroom teaches much about death and separation. Although autumn is a constant reminder of our own mortality, the hopeful concept that life is hidden within death is quite an indication of our final victory.

Jesus said, "I am the resurrection and the life. The one who believes in me will live, even though they die" (John 11:25, NIV). Let these words comfort and guide us. Let God's promises shake off the "whys" and "what-ifs" and fill our hearts with hope and faith to capacity.

> Very truly I tell you, whoever hears my word and believes him who sent me has eternal life and will not be judged but has crossed over from death to life.
> —John 5:24, NIV

October

The Bittersweet Glories of Winter

I haven't been outside much these past few days, but the sun-drenched afternoon under clear sapphire skies beckons, and I decide to venture out.

The bittersweet glories of winter have much to teach us. And how quickly nature seems to undress and re-dress itself out of its season-woven garments. For how different things look today from just a few days ago! Crisp breezes are dismantling trees of their final glories, blowing their remaining leaves this way and that way, sending them whirling to the ground or swirling in mid-air, like some graceful ballerinas in their concluding acts. There are wilted bushes everywhere and pots of lifeless annuals that only yesterday were bustling with life. The cycle of seasons is unstoppable. We ride our yesterdays as we rush forward toward our tomorrows.

> It is the believer's assurance of eternal life.
> The sun can rise and set, seasons can come and go,
> but in God there is no change.

The passing of time is a frightful concept for the not-so-young. We are incapable of comprehending eternity, yet we do not accept finitude. As our hearts yearn for life without end, the assurance of God's immutability speaks security to our very beings. It is the believer's assurance of eternal life. The sun can rise and set, seasons can come and go, but in God there is no change. He is unchangeable in His promises. He is the Source and Sustainer of life (see John 11:25; 1 John 5:12).

Reflect

❧ How is God demonstrating His unchanging nature to me today?

_____

_____

_____

I the LORD
do not change.
So you, the descendants
of Jacob,
are not destroyed.
—Malachi 3:6, NIV

WELCOME

November

But there is always a November space
after the leaves have fallen
when she felt it was
almost indecent to intrude on the woods
. . . for their glory terrestrial had departed
and their glory celestial of spirit and purity
and whiteness had not yet come upon them.
—L. M. Montgomery

November

The Lord Looks at the Heart

For some time, I had been admiring a particularly lovely tree I passed by on my morning walks throughout the neighborhood. Crows, doves, and a variety of other birds seemed to prefer it as well. It seemed to be a social gathering place for them; its canopy was a stop where they mingled and congregated as one big family in a ruckus of merriment.

It was difficult to pass by this tree and not pause, enthralled as I was by the gurgling calls and grating sounds coming from luxuriant, leafy branches. But then, almost overnight, the new season arrived. Tiptoeing through the hours of our days came the fall, tinting foliage in bright yellows and antique browns. Then frost and bitter winds huffed and puffed, stripping trees of their leaves, leaving outstretched branches exposed.

The birds, however, seemed to keep their usual gathering in their awesome tree. Through leafless branches and a thinner canopy, their merriment was now louder, their party flashier. I stopped one morning to observe this tree house of birds now that the view was improved by the changing season, and, to my absolute astonishment, discovered how mistaken I'd been all this time. For the joyful ruckus of birds had never really come from the lovely tree I had been watching but rather from the less attractive and smaller one adjacent to it.

> In today's world of selfies and social media,
> we are biased—more than ever.

I had made a common mistake. In today's world of selfies and social media, we are biased—more than ever—in favor of attractive physical attributes. Sadly, we often make choices, only to realize later that our expectations may have failed us again.

How wonderful it is to know that God doesn't focus on our outward appearance when it comes to our salvation or our relationship with Him! What matters most to Him is our heart and how we respond to His amazing love.

Reflect

∾ How can I encourage someone today with the knowledge that God does not show partiality?

_____

_____

_____

∾ Today I am thankful for:

_____

_____

_____

God's Words

"For God shows no partiality" (Romans 2:11, ESV).

November

No Room for Doubt

November has brought upon us the northern winds—crisp, frozen winds blowing leaves in gentle currents of nostalgia. Winds whispering songs from the past. Winds casting the land into a deep sleep.

I wish to hear God's voice in the strong resonance of the wind, see Him shine bright like the moon over the garden, but all I sense is His almost palpable silence.

Like Elijah, we ask God for physical answers. We want to hear Him speak in a clear, loud voice, but He usually chooses to speak through His silence. God spoke to Elijah, not in the power of the wind, earthquake, or fire, but in a still, small Voice. A Voice so still yet so clear that it left no room for doubt.

A Voice so still yet so clear that it left no room for doubt.

The winds of November have eroded the anatomy of the land. The garden has become a shadowy place even during the day. Yet there remains an essence of life in it that cannot be put to death. The same is true with God. He might choose to communicate with His earthly children in the hushed voice of silence, yet He remains a source of quiet hope and assurance so overwhelming that it cannot pass unnoticed.

Talking to the Father
Father, teach me how to quiet the voices of my anxious heart so that I can learn to hear Your quiet voice.

Mother Teresa said, "The beginning of prayer is silence. If we really want to pray we must first learn to listen, for in the silence of the heart God speaks. And to be able to see that silence, to be able to hear God we need a clean heart; for a clean heart can see God, can hear God, can listen to God; and then only from the fullness of our heart can we speak to God. But we cannot speak unless we have listened, unless we have made that connection with God in the silence of our heart."

> The LORD said, "Go out and stand on the mountain in the presence of the LORD, for the LORD is about to pass by." Then a great and powerful wind tore the mountains apart and shattered the rocks before the LORD, but the LORD was not in the wind.
> —1 Kings 19:11, NIV

Four O'Clock

It's four o'clock. The slanted light of November shrouds my world in gentle solitude. It pushes through naked branches and pours through the windows, imbuing the house with a sense of purity. It brightens my heart and washes my spirit clean in joyful feelings.

Light must have been blessed by God since the beginning as a special gift to all living things. In the cool days of autumn, its healing qualities place renewed thoughts into the mind, imparting new hope and a new vision of life.

The November light is a healing kind of light, one that pulls me outside at all times of the day and urges me to find refuge in its captivating, gentle glow.

I love how the world appears under the golden light of November. I love how the birds seem to flitter, swathed in a new joyfulness under their wings as they congregate by the bird feeders. How lovely! How marvelous this light is!

It is no wonder Scripture refers to Jesus as the Light of the world. He comes into our life, filling it up with little bits of joy, like sparkles of glitter, changing it forever.

> I am the light of the world. Whoever follows me will never walk in darkness, but will have the light of life.
> —John 8:12, NIV

Talking to the Father
Dear heavenly Father, how dark our world would be without You!

Caroline May wrote,

> And November sad.—a psalm
> Tender. trustful, full of balm,
> Thou must breathe in spirits calm.

The Full Armor of God

I knew they had finally arrived. A week ago I saw them gliding in the sky about the garden, proclaiming their arrival with their eerie, wailing call—a hollow *kih-kih-kih* that stretched over the horizon like a dark song. Two red-tailed hawks, male and female.

Soon they took possession of the garden just as they had been doing for the past couple of winters. But nothing could have prepared me for what I was about to witness that morning.

I heard the ruckus outside, followed by the hard thump of a bird striking the glass on the kitchen window, and, instinctively, I turned around just in time to catch a glimpse of the conflict taking place between a song sparrow and one of the red-tailed hawks. In awe, I watched as a flash of a high-speed chase followed—a vision of rich russet and gray feathers flying everywhere, until finally, out of that rubble came the impressive figure of the hawk lifting from the ground, carrying in his sharp talons the unfortunate prey.

I could not help but reflect on the warfare
that's taking place in the spiritual realm
and how what I had just witnessed in my garden
illustrates Satan's manifested enmity toward Christ's followers.

I could not help but reflect on the warfare that's taking place in the spiritual realm and how what I had just witnessed in my garden illustrates Satan's manifested enmity toward Christ's followers. The Bible tells us that we fight against spiritual powers. Our struggle is not against flesh and blood but against demonic forces. Our salvation resides only in Christ. The small sparrow doesn't stand a chance against the hawk, but let's not forget that the hawk and all of creation are under God's authority. We can stand strong under His protection.

Reflect

☙ Make a list of the armor God provides.

_____

_____

_____

_____

☙ How does the knowledge that other believers are also fighting this spiritual war encourage you to persevere?

_____

_____

_____

_____

God's Words

"Be alert and of sober mind. Your enemy the devil prowls around like a roaring lion looking for someone to devour. Resist him, standing firm in the faith, because you know that the family of believers throughout the world is undergoing the same kind of sufferings" (1 Peter 5:8, 9, NIV).

November

A New Heaven and a New Earth

Seasons interwoven—the end of one, the beginning of another. I am feeling a deep desire to be like swirling leaves, blown to that primitive Garden—a place outside this place. The land of all beginnings: Eve's Paradise.

As I walk the lonesome garden, its landscape becomes my soul, its wintry topography the landscape of my own heart, bare and longing for a bounty of seeds and blooms. I am remembering and treasuring precious moments of the past. Tales of my own history mingle with newer stories of my children and their children setting out on their own journeys.

This is the season of memories and thanksgiving, family times and gatherings, but also the season of nostalgia and deep loneliness for many. I am back to the reduced chores of the late fall garden, and my naked trees are back to gloomy days and frozen northern winds.

I am caught between two sentiments: the beauty of silence and the unrestrained joy of chatter, family, the laughter of children, the embracing, and the whispering in tiny ears, "I love you." How do I choose one without rebuffing the other? Can I choose both? Because I need both.

God's Words

Then I saw "a new heaven and a new earth," for the first heaven and the first earth had passed away, and there was no longer any sea. I saw the Holy City, the new Jerusalem, coming down out of heaven from God, prepared as a bride beautifully dressed for her husband. And I heard a loud voice from the throne saying, "Look! God's dwelling place is now among the people, and he will dwell with them. They will be his people, and God himself will be with them and be their God. 'He will wipe every tear from their eyes. There will be no more death' or mourning or crying or pain, for the old order of things has passed away" (Revelation 21:1–4, NIV).

WELCOME

December

In the bleak midwinter frosty wind made moan;
Earth stood hard as iron, water like a stone;
Snow had fallen, snow on snow, snow on snow,
In the bleak midwinter, long ago.
—Christina Rossetti

December

Booming in Faith and Hope

I imagined the angels had been at it again. Amusement-loving, mischievous angels who, just before the break of dawn, decided to camouflage the garden under a thick blanket of diminutive, sparkling stars. Some may know them as frozen raindrops, snowflakes that have become encrusted with ice, but it occurs to me that the ice crystals covering the roses and shrubs in my garden must be icy stars fallen from the bountiful treasury of God's ample pockets.

How can I do justice to the beauty and brilliance of crystalized snowflakes and to the God who rejoices in gifting us with unexpected beauty, just to watch how amazement grows in our eyes?

Certainly, God delights in our pleasure and is keenly aware of the intensity of human emotions and our need to recognize love with physical and visual representations. Unexpected beauty thrown at our feet is one of God's demonstrations of love. It is He knocking at the door of our understanding to remind us that He is a God who waits upon us, upon our desire of Him, that we may seek Him and surrender to His affection.

> Unexpected beauty thrown at our feet
> is one of God's demonstrations of love.

I like how George Washington Carver expressed it: "I love to think of nature as an unlimited broadcasting station, through which God speaks to us every hour, if we will only tune in."

Talking to the Father
Dear Lord, open my eyes to the beauty around me so that in seeing it, my heart may be prompted to seek You. Amen.

God's Words
"Yet the LORD longs to be gracious to you;
    therefore, he will rise up to show you compassion.
For the LORD is a God of justice.
    Blessed are all who wait for him!" (Isaiah 30:18, NIV).

Living Passionately

Daylight is but a passing butterfly these days. By midafternoon the slanting grayish-yellow light that settles over the dry grass is already staging the final act of the day. Just a few more minutes and the deeper amber glow of the setting sun will signal the demise of another day. Those last few minutes of daylight in the garden are precious to me, and many times I will race outside just before nightfall, braving the cold, just to witness nature's ritual.

I have learned to appreciate and value light almost as much as those who live inside the arctic circle. They who must cope with long, dark polar nights know they don't have a moment of daylight to waste. Summers are spent trekking in the mountains, boating, bike riding, and sunbathing. Even at midnight there are people enjoying the sun. It seems that they are intent on storing up as much happy sunshine as possible to help them live through their winters with enthusiasm, until the return of the sun the following spring.

> Teach us to number our days and recognize how few they are; help us to spend them as we should.
> —Psalm 90:12, TLB

Life is indeed short.
Therefore, it must be lived passionately.

The short days of winter remind me of how fleeting life is. Life is indeed short. Therefore, it must be lived passionately. Appreciate it. Look for the beauty in everything. The apostle Paul reminds us we should "never be lacking in zeal" (Romans 12:11, NIV). God wants us to learn to draw strength, hope, and peace from Him, the true Light of the world.

Talking to the Father

Dear heavenly Father, "in Your presence is fullness of joy; at Your right hand are pleasures forevermore" (Psalm 16:11, NKJV).

December

Magical Sparks

My eyes scanned again the desolated landscape of the garden, looking for any remnants of beauty, but my heart insisted in finding none. A cold wind swept the flower-barren garden floor in a crinkling sound of dried leaves, and my spirit shuddered. Winter depression had settled in. I lacked energy, and a heavy pessimism was depleting my last reserves of joy. I looked at myself, and, like with the garden, found no beauty either.

As I kept moving sluggishly through the winter garden, I pondered what God Himself would be seeing in me—a dull, uninspired, and uninspiring person. Then, suddenly, my eyes caught the cobalt flash of something gleaming beneath the edge of a stone. As sunlight passed through the object, additional colors were created with each new wavelength of light—from cobalt to violet to a deep magenta. What was it?

I hurried to investigate, and soon I was unburying the common and uninteresting piece of broken glass that, only a moment before, was casting such magical sparks of beauty and glory. Now, away from the ray of sun that gave it its beauty, it looked stained and dull in my hands.

I had to smile. For I, too, was like that piece of broken glass.

It is only under God's light that our true colors shine. We are forever beautiful to God. It's in our brokenness that we reflect the light of the One who shines with every color of the rainbow. Christ is the Light of the world. The God who can see through our flaws and shortcomings; and create light out of it all. God is light, and in Him there is no darkness at all.

Whether broken or whole, fragmented by the world around us or dancing on top of it, what we do with our lives depends on what we decide to do with the Light.

God's Words

"I am the light of the world. Whoever follows me will never walk in darkness, but will have the light of life" (John 8:12, NIV).

> Behold, you are fair, my love!
> Behold, you are fair!
> You have dove's eyes.
> —Song of Solomon 1:15, NKJV

The Heart of the Lover

How long had it been since I last visited the garden? I had to wonder.

My heart has been a tiny chickadee who deeply longs for this precious, dear plot of earth. Freezing temperatures and the heavy snows of the past few days have kept me away from it for far too long. Finally, today, I mustered enough courage to venture out.

A low, dark mist hugged naked trees and leafless shrubbery, obscuring the garden beneath it in cloudy sheets. In a way, the garden seemed larger and quieter, somewhat recalling the solitary expanses of open fields. I felt the pull of the land quieting my spirit. I felt humbled by what I saw and felt.

My heart is the heart of the lover when I'm away from this dear garden. At times, I like to believe it's a real, living, breathing thing, with a soul and a heart similar to mine. But in reality, it is not the garden who has a heart that counts its pulses in rose petals and a soul that feels and cries and knows how to love. This wonderful gift capable of eliciting such emotions comes from the heart of God.

> Therefore the LORD longs to be gracious to you,
> And therefore He waits on high to have compassion on you.
> For the LORD is a God of justice;
> How blessed are all those who long for Him.
> —Isaiah 30:18, NASB

> This wonderful gift capable of eliciting such emotions comes from the heart of God.

Does His heart yearn for us the way we long for those we love? Charles Wesley—widely known for writing more than six thousand hymns—could not have expressed it any better: "Amazing love! How can it be That Thou, my God, shouldst die for me?"

The father who is willing to die for his children would not abandon them. And neither would the God whose amazing, unconditional love for us sent Him to Calvary. Our limited human understanding can't possibly grasp how wide and long and high and deep is the love of Christ for us, but we at least have an idea. He waits only for our response.

Reflect

❧ How does the knowledge of God's immense love affect the way I live my life? How can I share this message with someone today?

_____

_____

_____

_____

❧ Today I am thankful for:

_____

_____

_____

He is the
Lover of my soul.

God's Words

"That Christ may dwell in your hearts through faith; and that you, being rooted and grounded in love, may be able to comprehend with all the saints what is the breadth and length and height and depth, and to know the love of Christ which surpasses knowledge, that you may be filled up to all the fullness of God" (Ephesians 3:17–19, NASB).

The Light of the World

December light has a unique feel to it. It scatters unfathomable reflections all over the landscape—jewels of goldenrod, ocher feathers, and mottled dead leaves—soft hues that must be interpreted in sentiments, for one must feel this light in order to understand it and appreciate it.

The defused goldenrod December light ignites the spirit and plays games with the imagination. It transports us to distant lands, and it dresses us in gowns of winter frost and garments festooned in twinkling stars made of ice and silence. This softer, weaker light can also bring forth in us a renewed yearning for God and the humble and heartfelt realization of our dependency and need of Him.

> I am the light
> of the world.
> Whoever follows me will
> never walk in darkness,
> but will have
> the light of life.
> —John 8:12, NIV

> We need Christ more than we need light to exist.

We need Christ more than we need light to exist. Without Him, our bones become brittle and our tongues dry. Our hearts turn somber. We need Him. We need the nourishment of the light of His Word, so that we may see and come to understand how wide and long and high and deep is His love for us.

Reflect
ꝏ How is Jesus revealing Himself to me in this season?

_____

_____

_____

_____

_____

December

Christmas Eve

Christmas Eve. It is cold outside. A light, powdery snow has been drifting down since early evening, blanketing rooftops and treetops in feathery-soft cotton. A cold wind runs through the empty streets, picking up the fine snow dust, and I marvel at how it swirls, creating a little dance around streetlamps and shrubs.

From my place behind the window, I think about the sacred story of that long-ago night in Bethlehem when Jesus was born. The wind outside throws a new puff of soft snow on the widow, and my imagination runs wild.

Our empty, quiet streets have now turned into the hills and valleys of Bethlehem. Out in the fields behind our house, shepherds tending their flocks of sheep have been awakened from their slumber by a mighty angel announcing that the Savior has been born in the town of David. Suddenly, the chorus of a great host of heavenly beings resonates outside my window, embracing the entire world with a new hope. They sing to God, to the shepherds, and to me and to you, proclaiming the good news that a Savior is born, "Peace on the earth, good will to men, From heaven's all-gracious King!"

The baby boy, Jesus, is the peace we need for our troubled world. Unfortunately, the world feels compelled to seek Him for only a few hours on a particular day. During those precious hours of Christmas, antagonism is put to rest. We sing carols of peace and forgiveness, even if it's only for a short time. We put ill feelings aside, bitterness and hostility to rest. We shake hands with estranged family members and share Christmas cookies with neighbors we haven't seen all year.

This Christmas feeling is so brief that we must hurry. Before the spell that brings the world together breaks, we must find that Baby Jesus. No time to lose! We must find Him before He gets tucked away for another year among the Christmas wreaths and garlands and the world gets back to its ferocious beating of war drums and pandering of fears.

Today in the town of David a Savior has been born to you; he is the Messiah, the Lord.
—Luke 2:11, NIV

Talking to the Father

Father, how far we are from You sometimes, when we forget to love, when we get caught in the tangles of this world and forget to love others as You command us to do. May we learn to love You and to love others as You have taught us.

December

His Glorious Gift of Salvation

This will be a sign to you: You will find a baby wrapped in cloths and lying in a manger.

—Luke 2:12, NIV

Dusk has settled upon the garden. The evening carries on its velvety arms the scent of wintergreen berries and wood fires. I want to stop the great clock of humanity and let the joy and the peace of Bethlehem percolate through me. With such thoughts swirling in my mind, I walk out into the garden.

I am welcomed into this cotton-white fairy-tale world, and I step into the snow-covered path that leads me to the small pine grove in the northwestern corner of the garden. I have come here countless times when the sun warms the earth in golden sheets of glory in springtime and when it is covered in bright colors under the rays of summer. I've come here in autumnal days, when the world gets dressed in garments of cobbler crust and brown sugar and cinnamon, and I have listened to the voices of angels in the songs of birds and the whispers of the longleaf pine under gentle breezes. But tonight, the grove is a special place where angels gather.

> But tonight, the grove is a special place
> where angels gather.

There is a particular loveliness all around me. The whiteness of the snow-covered yard enchants the soul, and in the wintry silence I want to hear the soft voices of the shepherds of Bethlehem as they tend their sheep. Intertwined with the song of the wind, I can almost hear a mother's soft lullaby as she rocks her newborn to sleep somewhere nearby.

I walk slowly, taking in the intoxicating scent of snow and pine, observing how the moon reflects off the ice on branches and rooftops. I savor every step, every star that shines above in the unperturbed sky. Then, under the canopy of heaven, in awe and admiration, I call upon the Christ child—my heart like an empty vessel, open and receptive to the Holy Spirit, until the miracle I've come seeking transpires. I am moved with His presence. He is all around me. I receive anew His glorious gift of salvation, offered to me from Bethlehem to Calvary.

Talking to the Father

If only we could learn how to keep You close to our hearts past the Christmas presents and the Christmas trees. Surely, Father, if we would only take You with us past the folly of New Year celebrations and every wish and resolution, we could make every day a day of forgiveness, glory, and joy and every turning point an opportunity to start again.

Reflect

∽ Reflect on God's recent work in your life.

_____

_____

_____

Draw closer
to God
in the new year.

Let the thorns alone, for they will only wound you.
Gather the roses, the lilies, and the pinks.
—Ellen G. White